SHORT TREKS ON CORSICA

About the Author

Gillian Price has trekked throughout Asia and the Himalayas but now lives in Venice and is exploring the mountains and flatter parts of Italy as well as the Mediterranean coast. Starting with the Italian Dolomites, Gillian has written outstanding Cicerone guides to walking all over Italy as well as Corfu, Corsica and Portugal. An adamant promoter of the use of public transport to minimise environmental impact, she is an active member of the Italian Alpine Club (CAI). Check her out at www.gillianprice.eu.

Other Cicerone guides by the author

Alpine Flowers
Italy's Sibillini National Park
Portugal's Rota Vicentina
Shorter Walks in the Dolomites
The Tour of the Bernina
Through the Italian Alps: the GTA
Trekking in the Alps (contributor)
Trekking in the Apennines: the GEA
Trekking in the Dolomites: Alta Vias
  1–6
Walking and Trekking in the Gran
  Paradiso
Walking and Trekking on Corfu

Walking in Corsica
Walking in Italy's Cinque Terre
Walking in Italy's Stelvio National
  Park
Walking in Sicily
Walking in the Dolomites
Walking in Tuscany
Walking in Umbria
Walking Lake Como and Maggiore
Walking Lake Garda and Iseo
Walking on the Amalfi Coast
Walks and Treks in the Maritime Alps

SHORT TREKS ON CORSICA

FIVE MOUNTAIN AND COASTAL TREKS INCLUDING THE MARE A MARE AND MARE E MONTI

by Gillian Price

JUNIPER HOUSE, MURLEY MOSS,
OXENHOLME ROAD, KENDAL, CUMBRIA LA9 7RL
www.cicerone.co.uk

Printed in China on responsibly sourced paper on behalf of Latitude Press Ltd
A catalogue record for this book is available from the British Library.

 Route mapping by Lovell Johns www.lovelljohns.com

 The routes of the GR®, PR® and GRP® paths in this guide
have been reproduced with the permission of the Fédération
Française de la Randonnée Pédestre holder of the exclusive
rights of the routes. The names GR®, PR® and GRP® are registered trademarks.
© FFRP 2021 for all GR®, PR® and GRP® paths appearing in this work.

All photographs are by the author unless otherwise stated.

Contains OpenStreetMap.org data © OpenStreetMap contributors, CC-BY-SA.
NASA relief data courtesy of ESRI

For Betty 'la courageuse' and dear Daddyo.

Acknowledgements
Many thanks to the late Walt Unsworth who first suggested I went to *la
belle île* and to trail mates Nicola and Laura for their great company on our
'island in the sun'.

Front cover: Marvellous Capu d'Ortu is on display at the village of Ota (Trek 2:
Mare e Monti))

CONTENTS

Map key 8
Overview map 9
Route summary table 10

INTRODUCTION 13
The treks 14
Corsica 15
Plant life 17
Wildlife 20
When to go 22
Getting to Corsica 23
Local transport 23
Accommodation 25
Food and drink 27
What to take 29
Waymarking and maps 31
Emergencies 33
Using this guide 33

THE TREKS 35
Trek 1   Sentier du Douanier: Cap Corse 36
Trek 2   Mare e Monti: Calenzana to Cargèse 45
Trek 3   Mare a Mare Nord: Cargèse to Moriani Plage 85
Trek 4   Mare a Mare Sud: Porto-Vecchio to Burgu 128
Trek 5   Mare e Monti Sud: Burgu to Porticcio 153

Appendix A   Useful contacts 172
Appendix B   Accommodation 174
Appendix C   Glossary of French and Corsican terms 179
Appendix D   Further reading 182

Updates to this guide

While every effort is made by our authors to ensure the accuracy of guidebooks as they go to print, changes can occur during the lifetime of an edition. This guidebook was researched and written before the COVID-19 pandemic. While we are not aware of any significant changes to routes or facilities at the time of printing, it is likely that the current situation will give rise to more changes than would usually be expected. Any updates that we know of for this guide will be on the Cicerone website (www.cicerone.co.uk/1059/updates), so please check before planning your trip. We also advise that you check information about such things as transport, accommodation and shops locally. Even rights of way can be altered over time.

We are always grateful for information about any discrepancies between a guidebook and the facts on the ground, sent by email to updates@cicerone.co.uk or by post to Cicerone, Juniper House, Murley Moss, Oxenholme Road, Kendal, LA9 7RL.

Register your book: To sign up to receive free updates, special offers and GPX files where available, register your book at www.cicerone.co.uk.

Note on mapping

The route maps in this guide are derived from publicly available data, databases and crowd-sourced data. As such they have not been through the detailed checking procedures that would generally be applied to a published map from an official mapping agency. However, we have reviewed them closely in the light of local knowledge as part of the preparation of this guide.

Mountain safety

Every mountain walk has its dangers, and those described in this guidebook are no exception. All who walk or climb in the mountains should recognise this and take responsibility for themselves and their companions along the way. The author and publisher have made every effort to ensure that the information contained in this guide was correct when it went to press, but, except for any liability that cannot be excluded by law, they cannot accept responsibility for any loss, injury or inconvenience sustained by any person using this book.

International distress signal *(emergency only)*
Six blasts on a whistle (and flashes with a torch after dark) spaced evenly for one minute, followed by a minute's pause. Repeat until an answer is received. The response is three signals per minute followed by a minute's pause.

Helicopter rescue
The following signals are used to communicate with a helicopter:

Help needed: raise both arms above head to form a 'Y'

Help not needed: raise one arm above head, extend other arm downward

Emergency telephone numbers
General emergency: tel 112
Fire service *(Pompiers)*: tel 18

Weather reports
www.meteo.fr

Mountain rescue can be very expensive – be adequately insured.

Symbols used on route maps

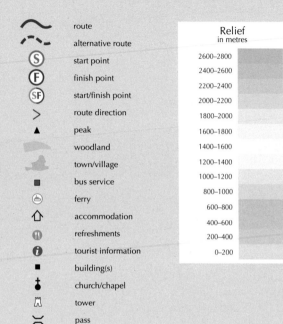

~	route
- - -	alternative route
(S)	start point
(F)	finish point
(SF)	start/finish point
>	route direction
▲	peak
	woodland
	town/village
■	bus service
⊕	ferry
⌂	accommodation
⑪	refreshments
❶	tourist information
■	building(s)
✝	church/chapel
⌂	tower
⋊	pass
=	bridge
•	water feature
✳	viewpoint

Relief
in metres

2600–2800
2400–2600
2200–2400
2000–2200
1800–2000
1600–1800
1400–1600
1200–1400
1000–1200
800–1000
600–800
400–600
200–400
0–200

SCALE: 1:50,000

0 kilometres 0.5   1

0 miles   0.5

Contour lines are drawn at 25m intervals and highlighted at 100m intervals.

GPX files for all routes can be downloaded free at www.cicerone.co.uk/1059/GPX.

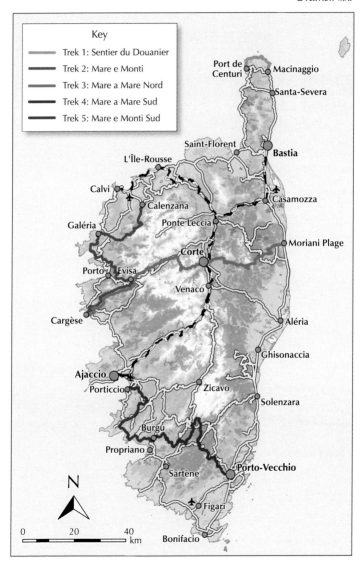

Key
Trek 1: Sentier du Douanier
Trek 2: Mare e Monti
Trek 3: Mare a Mare Nord
Trek 4: Mare a Mare Sud
Trek 5: Mare e Monti Sud

Port de Centuri
Macinaggio
Santa-Severa
Saint-Florent
Bastia
L'Île-Rousse
Calvi
Casamozza
Calenzana
Galéria
Ponte Leccia
Moriani Plage
Corte
Porto
Evisa
Venaco
Cargèse
Aléria
Ghisonaccia
Ajaccio
Porticcio
Zicavo
Solenzara
Burgu
Propriano
Porto-Vecchio
Sartène
Figari
Bonifacio

N

0   20   40
km

ROUTE SUMMARY TABLE

Stage	Start	Distance	Ascent	Descent	Time	Page
Sentier du Douanier: Cap Corse						
1	Port de Centuri	11.4km	500m	500m	4hr 15min	38
2	Barcaggio	13km	300m	300m	4hr	41
Total		**24.4km**	**800m**	**800m**	**2 days**	
Mare e Monti: Calenzana to Cargèse						
1	Calenzana	11.5km	560m	300m	4hr	48
2	Bonifatu	15km	800m	1200m	5hr 40min	52
3	Tuarelli	12.8km	230m	290m	3hr 50min	56
4	Galéria	11.5km	770m	800m	5hr	60
5	Girolata	10.5km	840m	550m	4hr	64
6	Curzu	8km	440m	700m	3hr 15min	67
7	Serriera	10.8km	1050m	780m	5hr 40min	70
8	Ota	11.5km	650m	260m	4hr 50min	74
9	Marignana	18km	825m	930m	6hr	78
10	E Case	13km	400m	910m	4hr 30min	82
Total		**122.6km**	**6565m**	**6720m**	**10 days**	
Mare a Mare Nord: Cargèse to Moriani Plage						
1	Cargèse	13km	910m	400m	5hr	87
2	E Case	18km	930m	825m	6hr	90
3	Marignana	15.8km	880m	120m	5hr 30min	94
4	Castel de Vergio	13.4km	160m	700m	4hr	99

Stage	Start	Distance	Ascent	Descent	Time	Page
5	Albertacce	12.6km	800m	450m	5hr 15min	103
6	A Sega	13.3km	100m	770m	4hr 15min	107
7	Corte	16km	1000m	700m	5hr 40min	111
8	Sermano	13km	650m	650m	4hr 45min	115
9	Pianello	13km	600m	750m	4hr 15min	119
10	Pied d'Alesani	9.9km	460m	530m	4hr 10min	122
11	I Penti	10.2km	50m	660m	2hr 45min	125
Total		**148.2km**	**6540m**	**6555m**	**11 days**	

Mare a Mare Sud: Porto-Vecchio to Burgu

Stage	Start	Distance	Ascent	Descent	Time	Page
1	Porto-Vecchio	17km	1000m	80m	5hr 20min	131
2	Cartalavonu	13.6km	600m	1000m	4hr 40min	135
3	Levie	18.4km	750m	510m	6hr	139
4	Serra-di-Scopamène	10.5km	400m	800m	4hr	144
5	Sainte-Lucie-de-Tallano	16.4km	670m	1120m	5hr 15min	148
Total		**75.9km**	**3420m**	**3510m**	**5 days**	

Mare e Monti Sud: Burgu to Porticcio

Stage	Start	Distance	Ascent	Descent	Time	Page
1	Burgu	10.6km	800m	650m	4hr	155
2	Olmeto	15.3km	350m	700m	4hr	158
3	Porto Pollo	11.5km	700m	300m	3hr 30min	161
4	Coti-Chiavari	16km	600m	400m	4hr 45min	164
5	Bisinao	13.5km	350m	1000m	4hr 15min	168
Total		**66.9km**	**2800m**	**3050m**	**5 days**	

A tricky rocky ridge is negotiated prior to the 700m saddle below Capu di Curzu on stage 5 of the Mare e Monti (Trek 2)

INTRODUCTION

Will there be anything worth seeing in Corsica? Is there any romance left in that island? Is there any sublimity or beauty in its scenery? Have I taken too much baggage? Have I not rather taken too little? Am I not an idiot for coming at all?

Journal of a Landscape Painter in Corsica, Edward Lear (1870)

From elegant Ponte Vechju you look inland to Monte Cintu (Trek 2, Stage 3)

In the quote above, poet and artist Edward Lear expressed his doubts about travelling to Corsica. He might also have asked: Is the food good? Are the wildflowers interesting? Are the guesthouses comfortable? And above all, are there any worthwhile walks? The answers to these questions are provided by this guidebook and are unfailingly 'Yes!'. There are hundreds of kilometres of marked paths, leading into marvellous rugged mountains and across crystal-clear rivers; to golden sandy coves by the brilliant turquoise sea; over scented maquis

scrubland, along old mule tracks, through romantic forests of majestic Corsican pine trees; and on to quiet villages offering accommodation in cosy guesthouses and friendly hostels. What more could a walker ask?

This guide is designed to give a taste of the delights Corsica offers, with its wonderful network of intersecting long-distance pathways that allow walkers to mix and match. Five time-tested trekking routes are enticingly described here in detail. However, two words of warning: despite the word 'short' in the title – *Short Treks on*

Corsica – two of these pedestrian journeys last as long as 10 and 11 days. (If it's day walks you're after, check out the Cicerone guidebook *Walking on Corsica*.) And secondly, they can be highly addictive: just one taste and you may find yourself back for more!

THE TREKS

The five long-distance treks revealed in the following pages ramble over the island from top to bottom with well over a month's worth of exploring. Well-marked paths cross a surprising range of terrain – from soft sandy beaches to grassy pasture and scrubland, pine forests and challenging rough mountain slopes, not forgetting river crossings. There's something for everyone; the (difficult) choice is yours.

The **Sentier du Douanier** explores Cap Corse in the island's far north. Short and very sweet, it starts at the pretty fishing haven of Port de Centuri and traverses solitary headlands and coves on the two days it takes to round the elongated cape en route to Macinaggio.

The outstanding **Mare e Monti**, Corsica's longest-standing trek, spends 10 memorable days getting from Calenzana to Cargèse. True to its name, 'sea and mountains', it's a roller-coaster of treats ranging from the breathtaking west coast to the rugged inland with its awe-inspiring mountain landscapes.

A hefty 11 days are needed for the **Mare a Mare Nord**, a superb coast-to-coast traverse all the way across the central northern midriff of the island, from Cargèse to Moriani Plage. Magnificent pine forests and landmark peaks give way to beautifully located rural settlements where time stands still.

Mare a Mare Sud links Porto-Vecchio with Burgu in five very enjoyable stages, crossing the southern realms of Corsica, touching on traditional mountain villages amid breathtaking rock landscapes and river after cooling river. This is probably the most straightforward of the long-distance routes.

Mare e Monti Sud is a relative newcomer. This five-day jaunt along the southwestern coast joins the beautiful gulfs of Valincu and Ajaccio, alternating beaches with hills, between the villages of Burgu and Porticcio.

THE GR20

Easily the most famous trek on Corsica, the GR20 lasts around two weeks and covers 190km. For experienced, well-equipped walkers, the challenging route links Calenzana with Conca, cutting across the island's mountainous interior. See the exhaustive Cicerone guidebook *The GR20 Corsica* by Paddy Dillon.

The inviting sweep of Cala Genovese (Trek 1, Stage 2)

CORSICA

Its shores lapped by the Tyrrhenian and Ligurian seas, Corsica is the fourth largest island in the Mediterranean – after Sicily, Sardinia and Cyprus. It has a surface area of 8682km^2, is 183km long and 83km wide, and is blessed with a stunning 1000km coastline. Moreover, two-thirds of its land mass is taken up by an ancient mountain chain punctuated by a good 20 peaks over 2000m, while one-fifth is forested. Since 1972, a regional nature park (the Parc Naturel Régional de Corse, PNRC) has been responsible for safeguarding a vast 3500km^2 central swathe of the island.

Corsica – or more correctly Corse, in French – is part of France, despite being closer to Italy in both cultural and physical terms, although in fact many of the inhabitants would rather be independent. A narrow strait of only 11km separates it from Sardinia, and it's only 90km across to the Tuscan coast, whereas it lies 170km from the Côte d'Azur in the south of France. The population of approximately 330,000 includes many mainlanders along with a sizeable percentage of North Africans, Italians and other Europeans. In contrast, it is said that more native Corsicans live in France than on the island itself.

Fanciful tales abound to explain the island's name. Phoenicians, the first seafarers to arrive, apparently referred to it as Ker-Cic, meaning 'slender promontory'. The Greeks came a little later and for them it was Kurnos, 'covered with forests'. Legendary Greco-Roman hero

15

Hercules put in here after labouring to fetch the golden apples at the world's end. He left one of his offspring, Kyrnos, in charge – another contender for the name. Perhaps the most colourful story comes courtesy of Roman mythology, wherein it belonged to a maiden called Corsa who had swum across from Liguria in pursuit of a runaway bull! Continuing this trend, to this day island life is infused with incredible accounts of miracle-working native saints at odds with ghostly spirits and gruesome acts of the devil.

Corsica's very first inhabitants are believed to have migrated from north Italy around 7000BC. These hunters and gatherers developed into herders, and were joined by later arrivals who left prehistoric menhirs and dolmens dotted through the hills. As is the fate of settled islands, vulnerable by their very nature, Corsica was raided periodically by Saracens and Barbary pirates, then occupied at length by the Pisans, who left some lovely Romanesque churches, and the Genoese, who stayed from the 13th century through to 1768, when they ceded it to France at a price, leaving a heritage of memorable citadels, watchtowers and bridges. In the meantime, island-wide rebellions had produced an enlightened period of autonomy under Pasquale Paoli (1755–69), concluding at the same time as the birth of Napoleon Bonaparte at Ajaccio. There were also limited periods under English

Statue of Pasquale Paoli, who led the island through a period of enlightened autonomy in the mid 1700s (Trek 4, Stage 1)

sovereignty, as well as occupation by the forces of Italy and Germany during World War II when soldiers all but outnumbered locals. A 1991 French statute granted the island limited autonomy, then in 2002 a law was passed, the *Loi sur la Corse*, giving the National Assembly greater powers and extending the study of the Corsican language. These days, 60 per cent of the population reportedly *parlà corsu* (speaks Corsican), and it is the essence of the *chants corses* (traditional Corsican chants) performed by the island's many talented singers.

Nowadays, place signs on the island are in Corsican as well as French – for instance Ajaccio and Aiacciu, Corte and Corti. The island's flag depicts a black Moor's head wearing a white bandana – this was originally a blindfold (a reference to the Moors' 1096 defeat by Spain), but was adopted by Paoli who transformed it into a symbol of liberation.

Appendix D suggests a selection of further reading material about the island.

PLANT LIFE

The island's striking plant life embraces magnificent forests of towering Corsican pines cloaking steep mountainsides, as well as myriad scented maquis shrubs – but there's lots more.

At sea level, the beaches are scattered with curious soft spongy brown balls, remnants of a flowering marine grass, *Posidonia oceanica*, king of the sea. As the broad fronds die and detach from the plant, they are broken up by waves, which roll them up and wash them onto shore. On beaches, the fronds also form thick banks which act as natural protection from erosion.

To see flowers, April is the best time for a visit to the coastal belt, although the floral show will be postponed if the spring rain is late in coming. Other seaside habitués are the showy yellow horned poppy which sports blue-grey leaves, and the crimson Hottentot fig, a native of South Africa as the name suggests, but now naturalised. The striking white Illyrian sea lily, the *Pancratium illyricum*, endemic to both Corsica and neighbouring Sardinia, flourishes from sea level to well over the 1000m mark.

Not far inland is the habitat of highly perfumed French lavender (*Lavandula stoechas*), its tasselled head distinguishing it from the better-known commercial variety. The divine scent of an astonishing range of yellow brooms is another constant on Corsica. More perfume comes from sweet honeysuckle, its creamy gold flowers draped over walls. An eye-catcher on otherwise bare rock surfaces is vivid purple and pink stonecrop.

Prickly pear cactus or Barbary fig (*Opuntia maxima*) produces bright papery flowers in spring, followed by sweet edible fruit for anyone patient enough to peel off the insidious spiky needles. Christopher Columbus is credited with bringing it from South America. Sailors carried it around the Mediterranean, as they believed the fruit protected them from scurvy and the leaves were applied to wounds to stop bleeding.

Towering giant fennel, or ferula, is a common sight on arid hillsides. Its tall dried stalks were once crafted into modest furniture and walking sticks, as well as serving as slow-burning torches. A sure sign of over-grazed terrain is the asphodel (*Asphodelus aestivus*), a tall lily-like plant with white flowers. The Greeks called it the 'flower of death', but on Corsica it was known as 'poor people's bread', as the starch-rich bulb was eaten widely until the introduction of the potato in the late 1700s. The dried plant is still used in rituals, and is widely held to be a powerful protector as well as an effective cure for warts.

The term 'maquis' refers to the scrubby vegetation band just inland from the coastline, with its subtle background scents blending rosemary with thyme, fennel and everlasting, and much else besides. It never fails to leave a lasting impression on visitors. For Paul Theroux, 'It smells like a barrel of potpourri, it is like holding a bar of expensive soap to your nose, it is Corsica's own Vap-o-Rub. The Corsican maquis is strong enough to clear your lungs and cure your cold' (*The Pillars of Hercules: A Grand Tour of the Mediterranean*, 1995). Guy de Maupassant noted that it made the air heavy (*Histoire corse*, 1881); while for Dorothy Carrington, steaming towards the island for the very first time, 'This is the scent of all Corsica: bitter-sweet, akin to incense, heady, almost, as an anaesthetic after rain...it is a perpetual and potent enchantment' (*Granite Island: A Portrait of Corsica*, 1971).

The hardy, woody maquis shrubs that thrive on sun-baked earth have hidden generations of bandits, and there are even stories of Roman soldiers getting hopelessly lost. Predominant is cistus, or rock rose, a straggly bush with small leathery leaves and surprising papery blooms in pastel colours of mauve, pink and white. A curious parasitic plant, *Cytinus hypocistis*, often grows at its base, its attractive yellow-red sheath resembling a mushroom. Another maquis standard is the strawberry tree (*Arbutus unedo*). This evergreen

Corsican hellebore; broom; prickly pear; Illyrian sea lily

is easily identified by its ball-like fruit reminiscent of strawberries in appearance, although not exactly in taste, and glossy leaves that resemble laurel. A member of the heather family, it is known on Corsica as a symbol of loyalty: according to legend, the shrub hid Christ when he was fleeing from his enemies; however, the traitorous heather did not hesitate to give him away and he was captured. The charitable strawberry tree was blessed with fruit. The heather was condemned to flower without ever producing fruit, although its woody stem is prized for pipe-making.

Other notables are the widespread shady evergreen holm oak, with tiny glossy leaves and small acorns, as well as the dark-green-leaved lentisc with clusters of red berries. Since time immemorial, its oil has been appreciated for treating problems of circulation and stomach ulcers. The bright myrtle shrub has delicate white blooms like hawthorn, and its wood is still used for basketmaking as well as for lobster pots, as it doesn't rot.

At a similar low-to-medium altitude, the vegetation band includes native Mediterranean cork oaks. Still important to the island's economy, they are a common sight, half stripped of their bark, leaving the bare trunk blushing bright red in its exposed state. The tough covering is non-flammable, a natural protection from summer bush fires.

Higher up, one landmark tree for Corsica is the chestnut – the island boasts 47 distinct varieties. Under Genoese domination in the mid 16th century, it became the island's mainstay. The traditional system for treating chestnuts was to dry them slowly in a typical double-floored *séchoir* hut, over a fire that was kept burning day and night. They were later milled for flour. A grand total of 35,000 hectares was under cultivation in the 1800s, although that declined after a blight in the early 1900s. Nowadays, it's down to a mere 4000 hectares.

The 800–1800m altitude range of the Corsican mountains – such as the Aïtone, Vizzavona and Bavella – are cloaked in magnificent forests of endemic Corsican or *laricio* pine. Often modelled into weird and wonderful sculptures by the wind, they can grow as tall as 40 metres and were prized by the Romans as masts for their galleys. Easily confused with the maritime variety, the Corsican pine has short rounded cones and dark bark with largish rough patches. The maritime, in contrast, sports deeply fissured bark, often crimson, while its cones are large and pointed.

Damp areas around mountain streams are home to the pretty lilac butterwort, its sticky leaves ready to trap insects. There's also the odd orchid, mainly the modest *Serapias*, better known as the tongue orchid, with pointy elongated petals in a rather nondescript burgundy-cream colour. A more striking orchid lookalike is the violet-green thick-stemmed limodore. Other notable wood-dwellers include pretty crimson-purple cyclamens and Corsican hellebore. This endemic has attractive drooping lime-green flowers, and its broad leaves were used by shepherds to keep their cheeses fresh, while the roots produced a valuable disinfectant for livestock. One final glorious showy flower is a rare sight in the mountains: the bright pink peony grows wild in springtime on the edge of forests.

For more, consult the beautifully illustrated *Wild Flowers of the Mediterranean* by M Blamey and C Grey-Wilson.

WILDLIFE

Thick woodland and impenetrable maquis do not facilitate observation of wild animals on Corsica – nor does widespread hunting. Quiet walkers in the mountainous regions can hope for at least a glimpse of the 'king of the island', the stocky goat-like mouflon recognisable by its showy curling horns. With a history stretching back 8000 years, this native of Corsica and neighbouring Sardinia has become extremely shy in the face of species-threatening poaching. Luckily, herds of several hundred mouflon survive in reserves in the Asco and Bavella areas and have also been reported by the coast on the Scandola promontory.

Much more successful is the *sanglier* or boar (*Sus scrofa*), its numbers around the 30,000 mark. In contrast to the long-disappeared native Corsican boar, which gave birth to two or three young each year, the well-adapted introduced species produce seven or eight offspring. Along with domestic pigs that are left to roam freely, they may be encountered in medium-altitude woodland in search of edible roots, otherwise you'll be aware of their presence from the trail of devastation they leave in their wake. Not even the avid hunters seem able to dent the population. Again, these are timid creatures, and the closest most visitors ever get to an actual boar is a hide left on a fence or the meat in a sausage. Both boar and pig are part and parcel of Corsican life – and cooking. In the legendary past, they even organised a revolution led by a talking pig, Porcafonu from Calenzana, who conducted discussions with the Almighty in favour of more humane treatment for his race.

Another 'success' story concerns small red deer. After they were shot to extinction in the 1960s, park authorities combined forces with hunters' groups to reintroduce eight deer from Sardinia in 1985. This number grew quickly and hundreds now fend for themselves in the Bavella mountains.

As for reptiles, Corsica does not have any life-endangering snakes such as vipers. On the other hand, walkers have a good chance of encountering harmless green/grey-and-black snakes which will not hesitate to hiss fiercely, a strategy that gives them time to slither away to safety. Other creatures of interest on the ground are the ubiquitous darting lizards and even geckos.

Roaming pigs are widespread

Last but not least, the enterprising dung beetles are worthy of a mention. Key creatures on an island where livestock is an essential part of the economy, they are encountered on pathways, often engaged in clown-like bickering as they industriously dispatch cow pats, which they roll away in balls for use as breeding chambers.

The best news relates to birdlife. The woods are alive with myriad finches, woodpeckers, and the dainty treecreeper spiralling its way up tree trunks in search of burrowing insects to feed its offspring. The curious migrant hoopoe swoops and dips over light shrub, emitting its characteristic 'hoo hoo' call, its distinctive black-and-white wings contrasting with its warm orange-nut-coloured body.

Magnificent birds of prey such as splendid rust-red kites are a common sight, gliding and surveying open mountainsides for small animals. Six to eight pairs of lammergeier (bearded vulture) are known to breed in Corsican high spots such as Monte Cintu and the Bavella massif. Known locally as the Altore (dweller in high places), this imposing bird has a wing span of up to 2.7 metres. Like the griffon vulture found in the central mountain ranges, it lives on carrion (such as mouflon and sheep) and is famous for its practice of dropping bones from a great height to crack them on rocks. Despite local hearsay, it does not prey on lambs – unlike the golden eagle, which is only a little smaller in size. Thirty pairs of eagles

21

thrive along the central mountain chain as well as in the easternmost Castagniccia. The eagle has a wedge-shaped tail whereas the lammergeier can be distinguished by its more slender elongated tail.

Acrobatic swifts and martins swooping and screeching overhead are a distinctive sight in the mountainous villages during the warm summer months. As the typical stone houses have unusually narrow eaves with no overhang suitable for nests, the birds often make do with cracks in masonry walls.

WHEN TO GO

The spring period from March/April through to May/June can be simply divine for the coastal and low-altitude routes, and this is also a perfect time for wildflowers. However, to trek the mountains, it's best to wait until June, as snow may lie late. July through to August and September is superb inland. These months usually bring hot conditions along the coast, although there is often respite thanks to cooling sea breezes. In any case, start out early and take a break during the heat of the day. July boasts the highest monthly average in terms of sunshine, although combined with August it also sees 70 per cent of the tourist influx, so accommodation in popular spots should be pre-booked at this time. On the other hand, these peak months mean better public transport. In midsummer, be aware of the risk of forest and scrub fires (see 'Dos and don'ts' below).

The footbridge over Rivière St Antoine (Trek 4, Stage 3)

During the winter months, the mountains are usually snowbound. Walks at low altitudes can be lovely, although be aware that rainfall is heavier and few accommodation options are open (the majority function from April to October).

This ancient Corsican proverb may come in handy:

Arcu da sera, tempu si spera
Arcu da mane, acqua à funtane

which translates roughly as 'Rainbow in the evening, hope for good weather. Rainbow in the morning, fountains of water' – ie torrential rain!

GETTING TO CORSICA

Air

Flights to Corsica may entail a stop-over in Paris before proceeding to Bastia in the east (best for the Sentier du Douanier) or Ajaccio (not far from where the Mare a Mare Nord begins), although a host of direct flights from all over Europe also land at Calvi on the west coast (perfect for the Mare e Monti start) as well as Figari near Bonifacio (handy for the Mare a Mare Sud and Mare e Monti Sud treks).

Sea

Ferries ranging from gigantic container-like vessels through to sleek, fast catamarans link the French mainland ports of Marseille and Nice all year round with Bastia and Ajaccio. These are supplemented by summer services to resort towns l'Île Rousse and Propriano on the west coast, along with Porto-Vecchio in the east. The majority carry vehicles as well as passengers. From Italy, the main ports of departure are Genoa and Livorno, with ferries bound for Bastia and Porto-Vecchio. The main shipping lines are Corsica Ferries (www.corsicaferries.com) and Moby Lines (www.mobylines.com). Advance booking for vehicles is recommended in summer.

LOCAL TRANSPORT

Corsica is fairly easy to get around by public transport – as long as you're not in a hurry: bear in mind that tortuous roads and summer tourist traffic may mean the odd delay.

Bus and taxi

A long list of private companies run minibuses and long-distance coaches (referred to as *autocars* or simply *cars*) all over the island. For routes and timetables, visitors need go no further than the excellent website www.corsicabus.org, which has them all.

Tourist offices in key towns such as Bastia and Ajaccio (see Appendix A) also distribute exhaustive lists of lines relevant to their region. Tickets are generally sold on board the buses. Most villages have a taxi service – ask at the nearest café.

See the glossary in Appendix C for some terms that may be helpful in deciphering timetables.

Ferry is the best way to get to Ajaccio at the end of the Mare e Monti Sud (Trek 5, Stage 5)

Ferry

Local ferries are handy as well as enjoyable, and can be used during Trek 1 and at the end of Trek 5.

Train

The train is handy for walkers heading for Calvi and the Mare e Monti trail, and is the perfect leisurely means of transport to reach Corte, a strategic point on the Mare a Mare Nord. The Chemins de Fer de la Corse, alias *U Trinighellu* or the *micheline*, is a marvellous narrow-gauge railway line that runs through the mountainous centre of Corsica connecting Bastia and Ajaccio, with a branch line to Calvi. A must for train buffs and everyone else, it makes for a memorable trip and used to be irreverently referred to as the island's TGV – *Train à Grandes Vibrations*! Pocket timetables are widely available, otherwise visit www.cf-corse.corsica. The line originally extended down the eastern seaboard to Porto-Vecchio, but the track was damaged by bombing during World War II and was unfortunately never rebuilt.

The most thrilling stretch of track negotiates the narrow valley between the stations of Corte and Vizzavona, with a spectacular succession of viaducts, switchbacks and tunnels, looping back on itself for the climb to the 1000m mark. Renowned French civil engineer Gustave Eiffel was responsible for the 1888 design of the noteworthy steel girder bridge in the proximity of Vivario station.

Car

A car is not especially helpful for trekkers as it's complicated trying to collect it at the end of your route. In any case, rental agencies are plentiful in the main towns and ports, although of course you can bring your own vehicle by ferry (with the appropriate paperwork and insurance). The French road identification system uses the letter N for the more important *nationale* routes and D for relatively minor *départementale* roads, plus a distinguishing number.

ACCOMMODATION

Trekkers will appreciate the excellent accommodation all across the island. That wonderful French invention, the *gîte d'étape* or walkers' hostel, is widespread throughout Corsica. Unfailingly great places to meet people, they provide excellent food and good sleeping facilities – usually basic dormitories with four to six comfortable bunk beds – along with shared bathrooms that always have a hot shower. You'll need your own towel and sleeping sheet (duvets or blankets are provided), unless you opt for a *chambre*, a private room with bed linen and towels and possibly an en suite, available at increasing numbers of *gîtes* these days.

Most establishments offer free Wi-Fi and also have heating if needed – a great boon for drying wet gear and keeping warm of an evening. Be aware that *gîtes* may not open until late afternoon, although a room will usually be left open for guests until the manager arrives.

A multi-course evening meal is served, very welcome at the end of a day's trekking. Guests eat together,

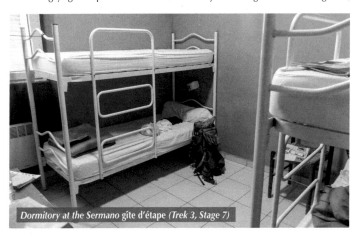

Dormitory at the Sermano gîte d'étape (Trek 3, Stage 7)

often at long trestle tables, which makes for a great atmosphere. *Dîner* generally consists of an *entrée* (starter) then *plat du jour* (day's special) and dessert. *Boissons* (drinks) are usually charged for separately. *Petit déjeuner* (breakfast) tends to be continental style – a cup or bowl of *café au lait*, *thé* or *chocolat* (milky coffee, tea or hot chocolate) served with *pain*, *beurre* and *confiture* (bread, butter and jam). Many places also have a *coin cuisine* (self-catering facilities), for which a small fee may apply. Should you require breakfast before the official time, don't hesitate to ask, as some helpful places will lay out the food beforehand and leave you to make your own hot drink. In any case, it's always good practice to settle your bill in the evening to save precious time the day after. Lastly, you may also like to order a *panier-repas* (packed picnic lunch).

Gîtes d'étape are mostly open from April to October, although this can vary. Some have email or a website for advance booking, otherwise phone to reserve a few days ahead – further ahead at peak holiday times. All are listed with contact information in the relevant trek stages and in Appendix B.

Lists of contact details for *hébergements* (accommodation) on the treks are updated each year by the Parc Naturel Régional de Corse (PNRC): see www.pnr.corsica/les-randonnees-decouverte and click on 'ce fichier'. Another handy site is www.gites-refuges.com.

After many nights in a communal dormitory, you may feel the need to treat yourself to a little luxury. Hotels and *maisons/chambres d'hôtes* (B&Bs that usually do dinner – but do check when booking) provide alternatives to the *gîtes d'étape*. These, too, are listed in the relevant trek stages as well as in Appendix B.

If booking accommodation by phone, bear in mind that a smattering of French will go a long way, and that Italian won't go amiss either as it is similar to the Corsican language. Landline numbers start with 04, and mobiles with 06 or 07. (If calling from overseas, preface phone numbers with +33, France's international dialling code, and remove the '0'.)

Charges at *gîtes* start at around €20 for bed only, and are in the €45–50 range for *demi-pension* (half board), which covers accommodation, dinner and breakfast. A little more is obviously charged for private rooms. Carry plenty of cash in euros on these long-distance routes as very few *gîtes d'étape* or even hotels for that matter accept credit cards. Where credit cards are accepted, this is indicated in the accommodation details provided in the trek stages, although to be on the safe side it's best to check when you make your booking. ATMs are plentiful in tourist towns, mostly on the coast, but are as rare as hen's teeth in the inland villages. Be warned!

Lastly, dotted across the uplands are *refuges* (mountain huts) run by the PNRC. The only one used during

The dining room at the Burgu gîte d'étape (Trek 4, Stage 5; Trek 5, Stage 1)

these treks is Refuge A Sega (Mare e Monti, Stage 5), akin to a *gîte*.

If you don't mind the extra weight, a tent and sleeping bag can provide a cheap holiday. While wild camping is not permitted along these long-distance routes or in the realms of the Parc Naturel, you can pitch your tent for a modest fee in the immediate vicinity of any *gîtes d'étape* that have an *aire de bivouac* (camping area), and can enjoy full use of the *gîte* facilities. Corsica also has a multitude of camping grounds dotted around the island. Contact local tourist offices for details: see Appendix A.

FOOD AND DRINK

The island's cooking tends to be basically French in the main tourist centres, but has retained its local flavour in the mountain villages. On the coast, you'll hopefully be able to dine on delicious *soupe de poisson*, creamy fish soup served with garlic-rubbed croutons and a mayonnaise-mustard sauce, then topped with grated cheese. *Civet de sanglier* (boar stew) needs to be tasted at least once. Corsica's unusual and invariably tasty cheeses include tangy rich *fromage de brebis* made with ewe's milk and smothered in dried maquis herbs, and the drier *fromage de chèvre* (goat's cheese). They may be served with fig conserve and even walnuts to cut the saltiness. In contrast, soft white *brocciu* is flavoured with wild mint and used in pastries or cannelloni.

The islanders have made some interesting adaptations to French specialities – *pâté*, for example, was traditionally made with blackbirds, although this practice is strictly for-bidden nowadays. In the charcuterie range, *figatellu* (pork liver sausage) should be on your list.

Vegetarians will have a little trouble, as the majority of Corsican dishes are meat-based. However, in the south, look out for *aubergines à la Bonifacienne*, eggplant stuffed with soft cheese and herbs and baked with tomato. Otherwise, ask *Est-ce qu'il y a quelque chose sans viande?* (Is there anything without meat?), or tell them you're vegetarian: *Je suis végétarien* (*végétarienne* if female). *Crudités* will get you a plate of fresh vegetables, and omelettes are regular fare. Traditional *soupe corse* (Corsican soup) is another good bet, invariably hearty and laden with garlic, beans and vegetables.

Those with a sweet tooth will enjoy the delicate dry *canistrelli* bis-cuits, flavoured with aniseed. Many desserts incorporate *châtaignes* (chest-nuts), which are sometimes milled into flour for concocting luscious custards. One unusual speciality is *confiture d'arbousier*, jam made from the fruit of the strawberry tree, which grows abun-dantly in the island's maquis.

Tap water all over the island is *potable*, meaning that it can be drunk safely. Of greater interest is the excellent beer brewed on Corsica these days (and there's no shortage of French brands either). Wine, on the other hand, either hails from the mod-est but interesting coastal vineyards or is imported from the mainland. *Appellation contrôlée* is a guarantee of

Petit déjeuner *at the Pied d'Alesani* gîte d'étape *(Trek 3, Stage 10)*

quality. If a whole bottle is too much to drink, request a smaller *pichet* (carafe) *de rouge/rosé/blanc* (red/rosé/white). Lastly, there's the thirst-quenching soft drink Corsica Cola – in an eye-catching red-and-white can.

Food supply points on the treks are indicated in the appropriate place in the route descriptions. Very few *gîtes d'étape* sell groceries, so it's always a good idea to have durable reserves of, say, crackers, cheese and sweet biscuits to see you through in case local shops are closed. Many out-of-the-way villages without grocery stores are served by enterprising travelling bakers and greengrocers, who announce their arrival in the main square by blowing their horn noisily. While they are unpredictable, they do mean a great opportunity to stock up on fresh fruit and bread, not to mention unfailingly delectable pastries.

WHAT TO TAKE

The bottom line is – always much less than you think. Lightweight T-shirts, undies and socks can be rinsed out every day so you don't need to carry more than one change of basic clothing.

Some suggestions follow:
- comfortable medium-sized rucksack
- sturdy walking boots with ankle support and non-slip soles are recommended as they are safer on wet terrain and loose stones and help prevent twisted ankles; they should be neither too new (blisters!) nor too old (slippery!)
- lightweight T-shirts and shorts
- long trousers to protect legs from the scratchy maquis shrubs
- lightweight fleece
- waterproofs – either a poncho or separate jacket, overtrousers and rucksack cover
- sleeping sheet and towel
- drinking bottle
- snack food such as muesli bars to tide you over if a walk becomes longer than planned
- whistle, headlamp or torch for attracting help in an emergency
- trekking poles for balancing on stepping stones and hanging out your washing, not to mention diverting your rucksack load off your knees
- sun protection – wide-brimmed hat, high-factor cream and sunglasses
- swimming costume
- basic first-aid kit with personal medicine as well as antiseptic cream to treat scratches, and electrolyte salts to compensate for excessive sweating
- sandals or flip-flops for beaches and evenings
- a compass combined with the appropriate walking map is a great help should you inadvertently stray off the track
- credit card, and cash in euros
- mobile phone with adaptor and recharger

Bornes de sécurité *poles are common in southern Corsica; marker pole for the Sentier du Douanier (Trek 1, Stage 1); the Mare e Monti and the GR20 part ways (Trek 2, Stage 1)*

PLACE NAMES

Place names on the island come in both French and Corsican, and there can be disparities between maps and signposts. Small villages and hamlets are important landmarks on the long-distance trails; however, few have identifying signs and there isn't often anyone to ask. One unfailingly reliable system for finding out where you are is to locate the local cenotaph, as each village sent its sons to the conflicts France was engaged in, and the village name is always shown on these monuments.

WAYMARKING AND MAPS

Most paths on Corsica have clear waymarking, using a regular succession of short painted stripes on trees or prominent rocks, often accompanied by arrows and signposts and the name of a landmark ahead. The long-distance treks described in this guide all have orange waymarks.

The Facebook page of the Parc Naturel Régional de Corse provides regular updates about path and bridge maintenance (www.facebook.com/ ParcNaturelRegionalCorse).

A detailed contour map is an essential aid to any walk undertaken on Corsica. The relevant sheets from the blue 'Top 25' 1:25,000 series published by France's Institut Géographique National (IGN) are listed at trek headings throughout this guide. This series is on sale all over Corsica in newsagents and even supermarkets, not to mention in outdoor and map shops overseas.

At a stretch, the green IGN 1:100,000 series could accompany a long-distance route and be used for identifying distant ranges and landmarks, including villages, although these maps won't be much help for navigating.

DOS AND DON'TS

- Don't underestimate Corsica. The terrain is rugged, and walking on the island does not mean a stroll along the beach. Find time to get in decent shape before setting out on your holiday. You will appreciate the wonderful scenery better if you're not overly tired and will react better should an emergency arise.
- Don't overload your rucksack. An excessive load can also put you off balance on exposed ridges or during steep descents. Be honest – are you really going to read that novel? Are those extra clothes really essential? (Corsica is a relaxed holiday destination and the need for

'dressing up' is rare.) Weigh your full rucksack on the bathroom scales before leaving home (without forgetting to allow for food and water for a day) – if it exceeds 8–10kg, think again.

- Don't set out late, even on a short stage. Always have extra time up your sleeve to allow for detours, wrong turns and time out.
- Be flexible when planning your trek. Instead of rushing straight through, allow for rest days and breaks for detours to places of interest.
- Carry plenty of drinking water, although you'll nearly always get a refill in the villages as most have a public drinking fountain or tap. Natural watercourses abound; however, so does grazing livestock, so drinking from streams is not advisable unless you are equipped with a sterilising kit.
- Keep to marked paths and avoid trespassing on private property.
- Always close stock gates securely.
- Be considerate when making a toilet stop and keep away from watercourses. Derelict buildings or rock overhangs are also out – remember that they could serve as emergency shelter for someone! If you must use paper or tissues, carry it away; the small lightweight bags used by dog owners are perfect. There is no excuse for leaving unsightly toilet paper anywhere.
- Likewise take all rubbish away with you. Even organic waste such as apple cores is best not left lying around as it can upset the diet of animals and birds and spoil things for other visitors.
- Don't forget adequate protection from the sun, which can be fierce when you're trekking all day.
- Don't underestimate sunstroke.
- Don't rely on your mobile phone, as often there is no signal.
- Please don't pick any fruit or flowers.
- Never walk too far without checking for waymarking or signposts, as you may take a wrong turn onto one of the many livestock trails.
- Do make an effort to learn French – it will undoubtedly be to your advantage. Most Corsicans are already fluent in two languages and shouldn't be expected to speak English as well. Appendix C provides a glossary of expressions that may prove useful (mainly French but also some Corsican), including terms commonly found on maps and signs.
- Check weather forecasts (*météo* in French) before setting out and be prepared to adjust your plans accordingly: see www.meteo.fr and choose 'Corse' from the 'Région' menu.

- Should you experience one of the island's infamous violent summer storms complete with torrential rain, thunder and lightning, keep well away from trees, rock overhangs, caves and metal fixtures, curl up on the ground and get rid of metallic objects.
- Take fire warnings seriously and be prepared to modify your walk route accordingly. There is always a risk of forest fires from mid June to mid September, and paths may be closed. Don't put your life and that of rescuers at risk. Moreover, remember that lighting a fire out in the open is strictly forbidden throughout summer, although a total fire ban may be in force for a longer period. Warnings are posted on www.haute-corse.fr. If you are unlucky and are caught out by a fire, take cover in a watercourse or on a safe high point where rescuers can easily spot you.
- Last but not at all least, behave as a responsible walker and leave nothing behind you but footprints.

EMERGENCIES

For medical matters, EU residents need a European Health Insurance Card (EHIC). Holders are entitled to free or subsidised emergency treatment in France. UK residents need to check post-Brexit conditions. Other nationalities need to take out suitable cover. In addition, travel insurance to cover a walking holiday is strongly recommended as rescue and repatriation costs can be hefty.

The following services may be of help should problems arise:
- general emergency: tel 112
- fire service (*Pompiers*): tel 18
  Composer (un numéro de télé-phone) means 'dial (a phone number)'. 'Help!' in French is *Au secours!*

USING THIS GUIDE

The five multi-day treks in this guide are described in stages that correspond to a reasonable day's walking, each stage concluding at a village where accommodation and meals are available. The route summary table at the start of this book gives an overview of schedules.

All the routes are of medium difficulty and will require a moderate level of fitness, but no technical skill or specialist equipment – although some include mildly exposed stretches calling for a sure foot and a good head for heights. These sections are flagged in the trek and stage introductions. Be aware that adverse weather will increase difficulty and make even an easy stage arduous.

Each trek description is preceded by an information box containing the following key information: start, finish, distance, walking time, the relevant IGN 1:25,000 map sheets, and access to and from the route (by public transport where possible).

The path climbing out of the Aïtone valley (Trek 3, Stage 3)

In addition, each individual trek stage has its own information box giving start and distance as well as ascent/descent and walking time. Ascent/Descent is important information as, combined with the distance covered, it gives an idea of effort required. Generally speaking, 300m ascent in one hour is a reasonable expectation, although of course this will depend on the gradient and type of terrain.

The walking time is approximate and does not include rest breaks or time out for taking photographs or nature stops, so always add on a couple of hours to be realistic. On level ground, an averagely fit person will cover approximately 5km in one hour.

Intermediary timings are given in the route description.

In the trek descriptions, features that appear on the accompanying stage maps are shown in **bold** with their altitude in metres above sea level given as 'm' (not to be confused with minutes, 'min'). Compass directions (N, S, NE, etc) as well as directions right (R) and left (L) are also abbreviated.

GPX tracks

GPX tracks for the routes in this guidebook are available to download free at www.cicerone.co.uk/1059/GPX. A GPS device is an excellent aid to navigation, but you should also carry a map and compass and know how to use them.

THE TREKS

The old mule track in the Tavignano valley (Trek 3, Stage 6)

TREK 1
Sentier du Douanier: Cap Corse

Start	Port de Centuri
Finish	Macinaggio
Distance	24.4km
Walking time	2 days
Maps	IGN 1:25,000, sheet 4347OT
Access	Buses from Bastia run year-round to Macinaggio (the walk end), where a taxi (tel 06 11536864 or 06 33647059) will cover the remaining 19km to Port de Centuri. The walk can be shortened by taking the May–Sept shuttle ferry from Barcaggio to Macinaggio (tel 06 14781416, www.sanpaulu.com).
Note	Do not set out in summer with strong winds and high fire risk. Be aware that Stage 1 has a few short stretches with a little exposure.

The superb Sentier du Douanier or Customs Officer's Path (abbreviated as SD) explores Corsica's northern-most tip, the 'thumb' known as Cap Corse. While the opening has a few rough spots, on the whole the walking is straightforward, not to mention highly enjoyable, as it sticks close to the spectacular rocky coast and visits sandy cove after glorious sandy cove. Stage 1 sees very few other walkers, while the later leg to Macinaggio has become quite popular as a day walk.

Waymarking for the SD consists of low wooden poles and heaped stone cairns, supplemented by orange paint splashes on the second stage. The whole area is a nature reserve and wild camping is forbidden; accommodation is in comfortable hotels.

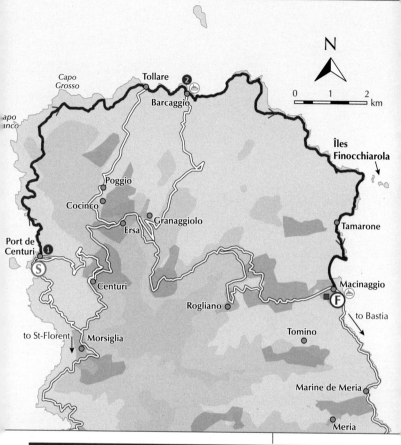

PORT DE CENTURI

The start point, Port de Centuri, is a cosy fishing village with a photo-genic harbourside lined with family-run hotels and restaurants frequented by yacht-borne visitors – this is France's leading lobster fishery. Accommodation options include Hôtel de la Jetée (tel 09 70356151, www.hotel-de-la-jetee-centuri.fr) and Auberge du Pêcheur (tel 04 95356014).

STAGE 1
Port de Centuri to Barcaggio

Start	Port de Centuri
Distance	11.4km
Ascent	500m
Descent	500m
Walking time	4hr 15min

The first half of this stage heads across rugged paths and saddles through scratchy bushes and over several narrow hands-on sections that can feel exposed. Once the north coast is reached, the going is easier and you drop in at the delightful seaside hamlet of Tollare; it's not far then to Barcaggio for a comfortable night at a guesthouse.

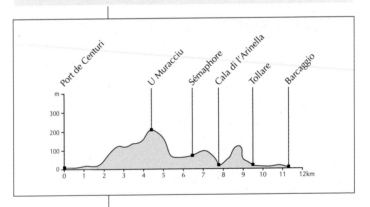

From the main car park and L'Auberge du Pêcheur at Port de Centuri, follow the steps past La Bella Vista restaurant then go R up to the church and road. A few metres further on, the SD forks L (N), soon passing an old wash trough. ◄ Scented maquis dominated by rosemary and myrtle shrubs accompanies the clear path via rocky coves. Some 40min along, after a sign warning of a *passage*

Above on the hillside are windmills old and new.

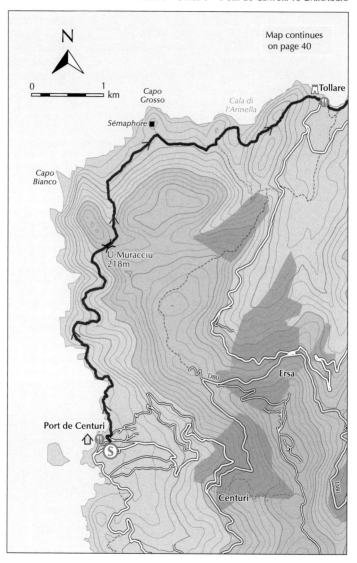

Map continues
on page 40

dangereux (ignore this fork), make sure you branch down L across a rocky gully following cairns, before a steepish climb over a minor headland. Long, mostly level traverses through bushes lead to the ancient stone wall **U Muracciu** (218m, **1hr 45min**), the highest point on the route, spanning a saddle inland from Capo Bianco.

Here, you look out to Île de la Giraglia. You're a little over halfway now – courage!

You drop to cross a stream and continue N in descent towards the sea, before a level traverse NE over dry red terrain colonised by hardy grasses. A helicopter pad precedes a minor road near the prominent **Sémaphore** (signal station) on Capo Grosso. ◄

Walk R (E) along the road for 1.2km to where the SD veers L to plunge to the quiet pebbly cove **Cala di l'Arinella**. Now brace yourself for the day's last effort – a stiff 150m climb to a crest-cum-lookout with a glorious view over the coast to Barcaggio, and Tollare with its watchtower at your feet. It's a stroll down to the photogenic fishing village of **Tollare** (**2hr**) where a rustic café and grazing cows await on the pebble beach.

A delightful coast-hugging path leads on E through shady woodland to masses of colourful Hottentot figs on the pale flat headland of Petra Cinta (encircled rock), surrounded by sea. Not far on is laid-back **Barcaggio** (**30min**).

Tiny harbour with café-restaurants and comfortable Hôtel Petra Cinta (tel 04 95368745, http://hotelpetracinta.free.fr).

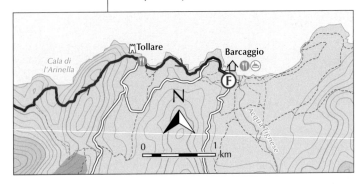

The Sentier du Douanier hugs the lovely coast at first

STAGE 2

Barcaggio to Macinaggio

Start	Barcaggio
Distance	13km
Ascent	300m
Descent	300m
Walking time	4hr

Today is a marvellous roller-coaster ramble via pretty coves, beaches and old watchtowers, and it all comes to a lovely conclusion at the well-served village of Macinaggio. If needs be, catch the ferry (see 'Access' information at the start of Trek 1).

Head E along the Barcaggio waterfront to join a road, then on to the SD sign pointing through to a car park. Here, a minor river is crossed on a footbridge and you're

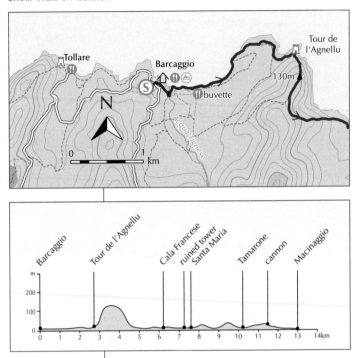

soon on the glorious sandy beach of Barcaggio, with banks of *Posidonia* interspersed with yellow poppies. Past a *buvette* (snack bar) are low dunes thick with elegant sea lilies. The SD rounds a headland through wind-sculpted juniper and cypress shrubs, touching on beautiful turquoise coves before the **Tour de l'Agnellu** headland and your first view to the Italian island of Capraia.

A short climb S to 130m is followed by a traverse W to inviting inlets enclosed by eroded light green rock. Sea lavender and rock samphire abound here, as do cormorants, and the sandy beaches of **Cala Francese** and **Cala Genovese** make perfect swimming/picnic spots.

The next interesting landmark is an attractive **ruined tower** (**2hr 30min**), then you reach fields where an

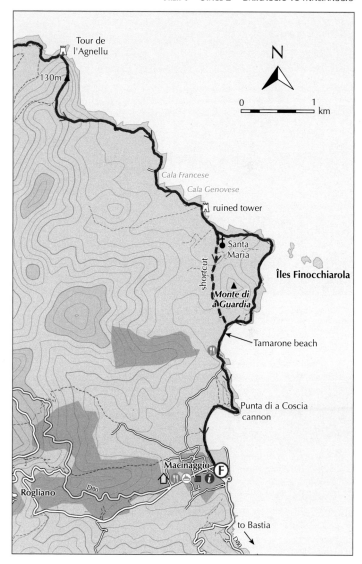

Tour de
l'Agnellu

130m

Cala Francese

Cala Genovese

ruined tower

Santa
Maria

Îles Finocchiarola

shortcut

*Monte di
a Guardia*

Tamarone beach

Punta di a Coscia
cannon

Macinaggio

Rogliano

D80

to Bastia

D80

N

0   1
km

The Sentier visits the Tour de l'Agnellu on its marvellous headland

Shortcut: from the chapel, a clear path heads S through fields, avoiding the climb over the Monte di a Guardia promontory and rejoining the SD at Tamarone beach.

Macinaggio was once an important port: muscat wine – appreciated by the papal court during the Renaissance – was shipped from here.

optional detour leads to the modest chapel of **Santa Maria**; if you visit the chapel, retrace your steps to the SD. ◄

Beyond a headland with head-high evergreen shrubs, the SD emerges to the sight of the Îles Finocchiarola, a nature reserve. Another stretch of sand (Plage des Îles) precedes a climb S over the promontory below Monte di a Guardia to popular **Tamarone** beach. Here, after the café-restaurant and car park, comes the final uphill section, initially on an unsurfaced road, before the SD breaks off L. You round Punta di a Coscia via an old **cannon** and walk along the beach to the marina and centre of **Macinaggio (1hr 30min)**. ◄

Restaurants, shops, bus for Bastia, tourist office and hotels such as U Libecciu (tel 04 95354322, www.u-libecciu.com). Camping U Stazzu (tel 04 95354376, https://camping-u-stazzu.jimdo.com, campsite with bungalows).

TREK 2
Mare e Monti: Calenzana to Cargèse

Start	Calenzana
Finish	Cargèse
Distance	122.6km
Walking time	10 days
Maps	IGN 1:25,000, sheets 4149OT, 4150OT, 4151OT
Access	A year-round bus from Calvi railway station runs to Calenzana. Failing that, try hitching a lift or take a taxi (tel 04 95627780 or 06 08165365) – the GR20 commences here so trekkers are plentiful. Villages en route can be used as exit/entry points: Fangu is on the summer Calvi–Porto bus run, as are Curzu and Serriera. Further on, Ota is linked year-round with Porto, while Evisa and Marignana have buses to Ajaccio. The novel (and only!) way to access or leave the isolated fishing hamlet of Girolata is by boat to Porto in summer. The finish point at Cargèse has buses to Ajaccio and Calvi.
Note	There are short, moderately exposed stretches in Stages 4 and 5.

The superb Mare e Monti (sometimes referred to as Tra Mare e Monti or TMM) follows a huge 'S' as it heads southwards, ducking in and out of the reliefs parallel to Corsica's rugged west coast. The many and varied highlights include the Forest of Bonifatu, the Fango river gorge, the isolated fishing village of Girolata, the Golfe de Porto and the Spilonca gorge, along with days and days of wandering through memorable maquis impregnated with the scents of the Mediterranean and bright with wildflowers. Don't forget to carry swimming gear for the rock pools, rivers and sea, as there are almost daily opportunities for a dip! Waymarks are orange paint stripes.

The concluding two days are shared with the Mare a Mare Nord route, so it's a good idea to pre-book accommodation at peak times. The trek can easily be lengthened into a rewarding 12-day route by slotting into Stage 3 of the Mare a Mare Nord at Evisa and branching eastwards towards the island's centre to conclude at Corte.

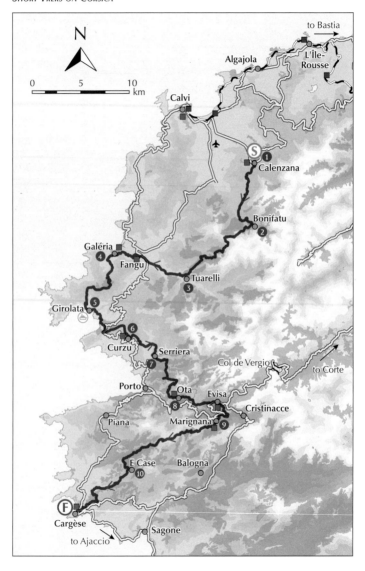

Calvi is a transport hub for the Mare e Monti

CALVI

Everyone passes through Calvi on the way to the trek start. This charming seaside town with a picturesque Genoese citadel (now occupied by the French Foreign Legion) is cleverly placed on a magnificent promontory, overlooking a colourful leisure port alongside a divine white sandy beach. A curious item of historic trivia: in the late 1700s during a siege of the citadel by the English under Horatio Nelson, the great man won the battle but sustained serious injury to his right eye.

Calvi has shops galore, ATM, as well as restaurants and accommodation for all pockets. Tourist office (tel 04 95651667).

CALENZANA

The trek start at Calenzana (or Calinzana) is a quiet spot these days, in contrast to its past as a hotbed of gangsters according to Ian Fleming (*On Her Majesty's Secret Service*). Screeching, swooping swifts bring the place alive in summer. It has a *gîte d'étape* with a camping ground, 5min on foot before the village (tel 04 95627713, sleeps 30, open Apr–Oct, cooking facilities). In the village proper are shops and restaurants, ATM, also comfortable Hôtel Bel Horizon (tel 04 9562717, accepts credit cards).

STAGE 1
Calenzana to Bonifatu

Start	Calenzana
Distance	11.5km
Ascent	560m
Descent	300m
Walking time	4hr
Note	A sign at Calenzana advises walkers on the Mare e Monti that they must set off on this stage **before 8am** from June to September due to possible fire risk.

A wonderful start to the Mare e Monti through the Balagne region known as 'the garden of Corsica', this stage has an initial stretch in common with the GR20. It takes you away from the agricultural flats backing the coast and straight up to a panoramic ridge with wild rocky reliefs, before heading into the beautiful Forest of Bonifatu. Here, a cosy hotel-cum-*gîte d'étape* is ensconced in trees, not far from a marvellous river swimming spot.

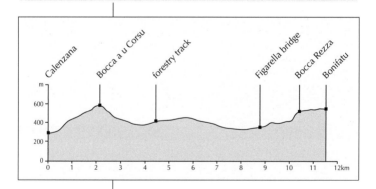

Coming from the Calvi direction, at the start of the village of Calenzana (275m), either fork R at the GR20 bar-pizzeria and follow waymarks to the supermarket, or continue up to the main square with its two churches

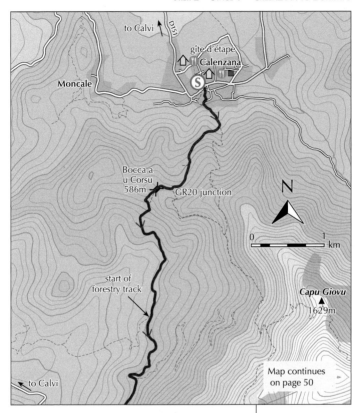

– here, turn R uphill on Rue Neuve then R below the Hôtel de Ville (Town Hall) to the supermarket, where you turn L. Plentiful waymarks lead out of the southern edge of the village and onto a paved path that winds and climbs steadily SSW through masses of heady herbs and flowers with the odd shady patch. ▶ At a **junction** where the GR20 heads off SE, keep R to follow orange paint splashes to the nearby ample grassy saddle of scenic **Bocca a u Corsu** (586m, **1hr**), where you bid farewell to the coast.

Sheep tracks criss-cross the slopes, and bright broom has colonised abandoned terracing beneath curious weathered rock formations.

Due S now, the path plunges down a wild dry hillside carpeted with scented broom and rock roses. Two stream crossings later, it emerges at a bend to join a **forestry track** (415m). Keep straight on in imperceptible ascent, with ample time to admire the accompanying blooms of the maquis shrubs, including the strawberry tree. ◄ Bearing E below prominent Punta Scaffa, it's then

These are the reforested realms of the Forêt de Sambuccu.

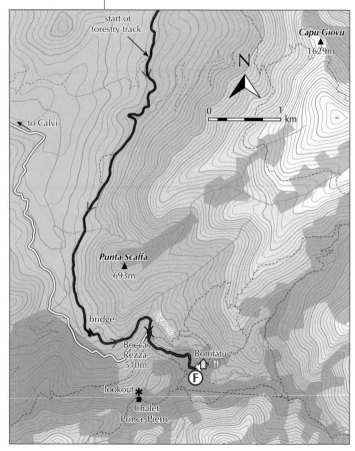

downhill past striking granite formations with views up to the peaks crowning the Cirque de Bonifatu, and to a **bridge over the Figarella** (360m, **2hr**), a boulder-choked watercourse with good picnic spots.

After crossing the bridge, the path (L) clambers briefly uphill across rocks before returning to the water's edge. Not far on are cascades followed by a prominent rock overhang sheltering Corsican lilies and cyclamen. Then the path turns R in zigzags to emerge up at the road and **Bocca Rezza** (510m). With an inspiring backdrop of pink granite mountains inland, turn L along the tarmac for the stroll across a stone bridge and past a car park to **Bonifatu** (535m, **1hr**). ▶

Set amid towering pines and boasting a shady restful garden, Auberge de la Fôret doubles as hotel and *gîte d'étape* (tel 04 95650998 or 06 50775636, **www.auberge-foret-bonifatu.com**, sleeps 32, open Apr–Sept). It has cabins and camping area, and serves delicious hearty cuisine; no self-catering.

Postpone putting your feet up and pop down to the river and the *pont suspendu* (suspension bridge) for a delicious cooling dip in the rock pools.

STAGE 2

Bonifatu to Tuarelli

Start	Bonifatu
Distance	15km
Ascent	800m
Descent	1200m
Walking time	5hr 40min

A tiring but rewarding traverse of the beautiful wild Forêt de Bonifatu, coming to a rewarding conclusion at an idyllically located hostel on the Fango river.

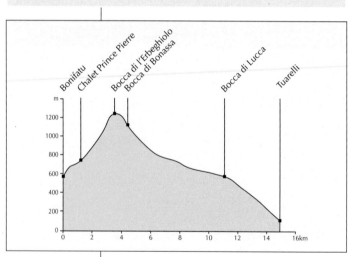

At Bonifatu, backtrack a short distance down the road to the stone bridge, where there's a signpost for the Mare e Monti. Turn L on the clear path, climbing in a SW direction through beautiful shady forest of pine mixed with turkey oak, via the odd clearing left by charcoal

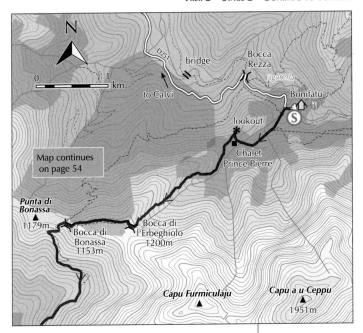

burners. Underfoot amid moss are pretty cyclamens and oversized Corsican hellebore plants, along with chaotic boar scratchings. Across a stream are the ruins of the so-called **Chalet Prince Pierre** (named after Bonaparte's nephew). Soon afterwards is a fine **lookout** over lightly wooded red granite mountainsides, with the Figarella river meandering to the coast.

Tree heather and maritime pines with fissured bark dominate on the ensuing zigzagging slog SW that finally concludes at **Bocca di l'Erbeghiolo** (1200m, **2hr**). ▶ The path continues L (W) in descent to **Bocca di Bonassa** (1153m, **15min**), which marks a surprisingly abrupt departure from the forest into the fragrances of the maquis, with plunging views opening up to the southwest.

Follow waymarks carefully on this section. The descent path due S is all but suffocated by masses of

Once you've got your breath back, enjoy the views all the way back to Calvi.

53

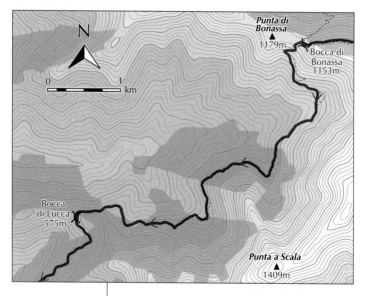

There are lovely views from giant rock slabs which double as great picnic spots.

lavender and hellebore for the initial dry tract; however, light woodland reappears as a constant companion, with even the odd chestnut tree. You bear SW and cross count-less streams in varying states of dryness. ◀ The next land-mark is the saddle **Bocca di Lucca** (575m, **2hr 10min**).

Now a slow but sure descent through shoulder-high rock roses, juniper and asphodels leads down to a quiet road. Turn sharp L parallel to the bank of the Fango river, where you can relax and put your feet up at **Tuarelli** (90m, **1hr 15min**).

Camping ground and *gîte d'étape* L'Alzelli (tel 04 956213882 or 06 20484986, l.alzelli.gite.tuarelli@ gmail.com, sleeps 24, open Apr–Oct, no cooking facilities). Before dinner, two related activities are compulsory: an invigorating swim in the incredibly transparent pools of the Fango river, followed by a refreshing beer on the terrace in the shade of olive trees, looking inland to the Paglia Orba.

The Tuarelli gîte d'étape has a shady terrace

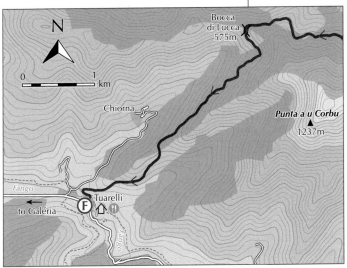

STAGE 3
Tuarelli to Galéria

Start	Tuarelli
Distance	12.8km
Ascent	230m
Descent	290m
Walking time	3hr 50min

You are led back to the coast today, and – in view of the relatively short distance to be covered – can enjoy the lovely natural rock pools along the course of the crystal-clear Fango, whose name, ironically, means 'mud'!

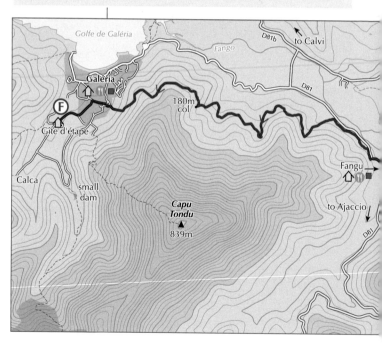

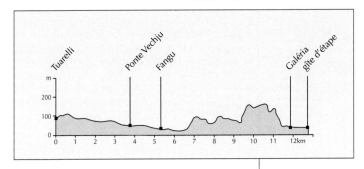

Follow the lane from the Tuarelli *gîte* along the Fango river downstream to a bridge over a stunning gorge, but turn R without crossing it. A short way along, a signed path skirts a property before following the riverbank

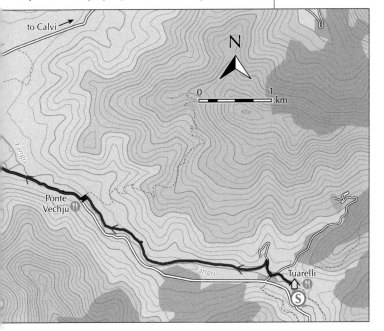

There are superb swimming spots amid the smooth orange-red porphyry rock-base, moulded over time by the patiently flowing water.

through waist-high rock roses and myrtle bushes. ◄ Soon in sight is **Ponte Vechju** (46m, **1hr 15min**), a superb elegantly arched Genoese bridge, stunningly restored to its former glory – your last chance for a dip before the sea.

Cross the bridge to a restaurant and pick up the D351 road R (NW) towards the coast. Some 1.5km along, past a drinking fountain and farm properties, is a T-junction and petrol station at the sleepy hamlet of **Fangu** (29m, **20min**).

A swim in the Fango river is hard to resist

Bus (Calvi–Porto service), snack bar, and excellent
restaurant with rooms Hôtel La Ciucciarella (tel 04
95332522, **https://la-ciucciarella.business.site**,
open Feb–Nov, accepts credit cards). Comfortable
B&B La Casaloha (tel 04 95344695, lacasaloha@
gmail.com).

Go R a short way along the D81 to where the
Mare e Monti turns off L immediately after a bridge. A
climb ensues into a canopy of tree heather, essentially
NW before a lengthy stretch of dry scratchy scrub sees
you through to a large water tank and rough track.
Maintaining the same direction, a path resumes for gentle
ups and downs and the odd watercourse, not to mention
cows.

You eventually climb past an abandoned shep-
herd's hut encircled by huge fennel plants. A **180m col**
is gained, overlooking the enticing coast and the delta
of the Fango river. Flanking an old stone wall, the path
descends easily to the seaside village of **Galéria** (40m,
2hr).

Shops, ice creams, restaurants and modest hotels,
including centrally sited Hôtel Camparellu (tel
06 71971048, **http://hotel-camparellu.galeria.
hotels-corsica.net**). A stroll away is a decent, if
gravelly, beach, as well as an evocative cemetery
with monumental family tombs silhouetted on the
seafront.

After passing the post office and church, follow signs
L (SW) for Calca along a quiet country road to a scatter of
farms and a **gîte d'étape** (30m, **15min**) in a relaxed rural
atmosphere.

L'Étape Marine is spotless and spacious (tel 04
95620046 or 07 86046455, sleeps 36, open mid
Mar–Oct, no cooking facilities, camping possible).

STAGE 4
Galéria to Girolata

Start	Galéria *gîte d'étape*
Distance	11.5km
Ascent	770m
Descent	800m
Walking time	5hr

Magnifique! One of the top days on the Mare e Monti, this sees you cross the scenic wooded ridge separating the Golfe de Galéria from the glorious Golfe de Girolata and dropping in to an isolated fishing settlement, accessible exclusively by sea or footpath. There's a very brief, averagely exposed passage in the middle section, slippery in the wet.

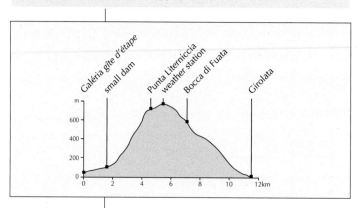

If you stayed at Galéria, follow the Calca road for 15min to the *gîte d'étape*.

◄ From the *gîte d'étape*, turn L (SW) along the road. After a bridge you are pointed L into scrubland to penetrate a lovely wild valley headed by red rock crests. Shaded by oaks and chestnut, the path crosses a watercourse, passes a **small dam** then goes back and forth across the stream. Heaps of old stone walls are encountered, overgrown with lentisc and rock roses.

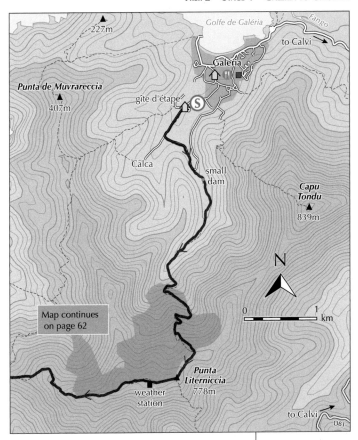

Map continues on page 62

At a large cairn there are lovely views back down over Galéria and a succession of headlands. The path winds up a little higher to a ridge, where you catch sight of the serpentine Calvi–Porto road and look inland to jagged rows of crests. Bear R amid thick cistus bushes to a prominent evergreen oak and signed junction (where a path breaks off L to the road at Col de Palmarella). This is **Punta Literniccia** (778m, **2hr 30min**). ▸

From here, there are wonderful views down to the bay where Girolata hamlet nestles, then over to Capo Senino and even Capu Rossu beyond.

Marvellous views inland include the distinctive shape of Paglia Orba (east-southeast).

To the west is a wild headland with deep red rocks, belonging to the protected Scandola Reserve.

Following the broad crest, the path continues climbing and bears W, with plenty of openings in the light cover of woodland allowing constantly improving views; shrubs here have been sculpted into bonsai shapes by the combined effects of livestock nibbling and wind action. ◄ The ridge narrows considerably, with a short clamber over exposed rock. The next landmark consists of antennae and a small **weather station** (775m).

The route finally begins descending easily through thickets of rock roses, overlooking the tortuous coastline with myriad inlets. An oblique descent leads to a semi-circle of stones on the ample saddle of **Bocca di Fuata** (458m, **1hr 15min**). ◄

The path drops easily due S then follows a wide ravine down to sea level. A lovely path turns L for the delightful last leg, coasting over divine green-blue waters towards the Genoese watchtower and haven of **Girolata**, aka Ghjirulatu (0m, **1hr 15min**).

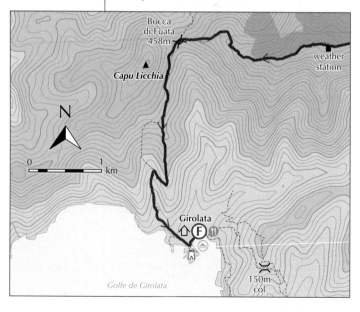

The path approaches Girolata

Modest grocery store, a handful of restaurants and two welcoming *gîtes d'étape*. Set just above the bay is comfortable Le Cormoran Voyageur (tel 04 95201555, cormoranvoyageur@hotmail.fr, sleeps 20, open Apr–late Sept, no kitchen facilities but freshly caught fish and home-made jam are served). Otherwise, a lovely beachfront restaurant, La Cabane du Berger, provides its guests with rustic timber huts shaded by eucalypts (tel 04 95201698 or 06 10230822, sleeps 30, open Apr–late Sept, accepts credit cards, camping ground). Summer ferries to Porto.

The fishing settlement of **Girolata** has a lively summertime population as restaurants open up and families return to cater to the boat-borne crowds, whereas in winter the figure oscillates between one and ten. The beach itself is a little scruffy and not exactly inviting, due to the resident cows and the fleets of motor boats and yachts that crowd the bay in high season. Put off your swim until Tuara tomorrow.

STAGE 5
Girolata to Curzu

Start	Girolata
Distance	10.5km
Ascent	840m
Descent	550m
Walking time	4hr

After dropping in at a lovely beach, you climb to the road before a stiff ascent via an elevated ridge with open rocky sections. All effort is amply recompensed by the sweeping views over the spectacular coastline. The stage comes to a fitting conclusion at a well-reputed *gîte*-cum-restaurant in a panoramic location.

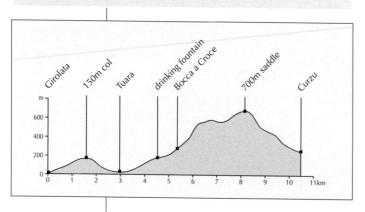

A longer variant to Tuara keeps R, closer to the waterfront, and entails a little clambering.

At Girolata, head along the eucalpyt-backed shingle beach with its jetties. At the far end, over a bridge, continue straight ahead up the orange-marked path. ◄ The path passes a tiny cemetery, bearing E to climb over slabs alongside a drystone wall amid shady shrubs, reaching a signpost at a **150m col**. Keep R (SE) here downhill for lovely **Tuara**, your last beach until the trek's conclusion!

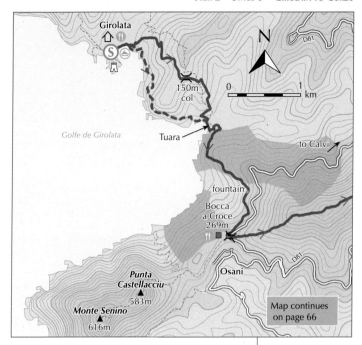

Towards the far end of the sand, turn inland for a wide path over a bridged stream and up into shady woods. This broad way (the former postman's route) climbs steadily S past a **drinking fountain** to emerge on the D81 at the snack bar at **Bocca a Croce** (269m, 1hr 30min). ▸ If needs be, you can bail out here, thanks to the Porto–Calvi bus.

With an eye out for traffic, go straight across the road and up past a radio mast for a stiff dusty haul ENE in the company of grasshoppers. You gain a broad panoramic crest with ever-improving views over the gulfs of Girolata and Porto, taking in spectacular Capu Rossu. Around the 600m level, the gradient finally eases and an open rocky ridge is negotiated – watch your step. Further along, immediately after a massive

Legendary postman Guy Ceccaldi, or Guy le Facteur, walked this path daily for over 20 years, a 14km round trip, to deliver mail to Girolata.

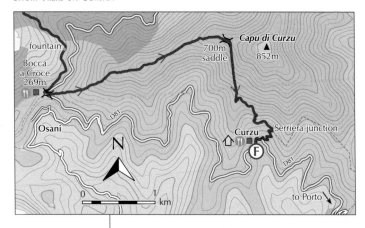

Mediterranean oak tree, is a **700m saddle (1hr 30min)** below Capu di Curzu. And here you're pointed R – in descent at last, cutting across dry hillsides.

The last leg to the village entails more tiring stony terrain and age-old olive trees. On the upper outskirts of **Curzu**, at the first houses, keep R at a junction signposted to Serriera (where Stage 6 turns off) for

The path descends across dry hillsides

a succession of steps and laneways past old stone ovens and a church to a drinking fountain and the D81 road once more. Keep R for the welcoming family-run **gîte d'étape** of Curzu (290m, **1hr**).

> The *gîte d'étape* has an excellent reputation for traditional Corsican catering (tel 04 95273170 or 06 22161593, **www.gite-de-curzo.com**, sleeps 42 in rooms and dorms, open Apr–Oct, accepts credit cards, camping possible) and enjoys a wonderful outlook to Capu d'Ortu. The Porto–Calvi bus can be picked up here. Some groceries available.

STAGE 6
Curzu to Serriera

Start	Curzu
Distance	8km
Ascent	440m
Descent	700m
Walking time	3hr 15min

Today's route is a straightforward traverse of hills clad in scratchy maquis and scrubby pastureland, ending at an attractive *gîte d'étape*.

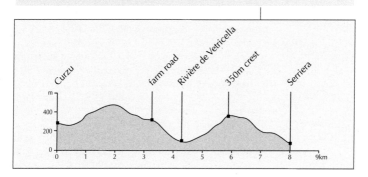

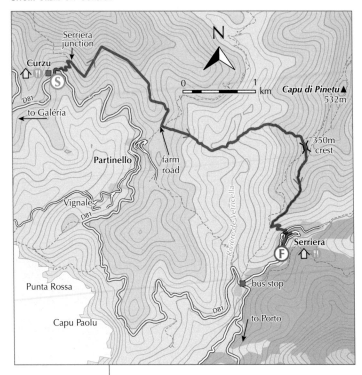

At Curzu, climb back up past the drinking fountain and church the way you arrived. Just below the last house at the junction signposted to Serriera, turn R (SE) on a goat track along overgrown terraces. Waymarking is constant but the going can be thorny – be warned! You coast above the cemetery and make your way past red rock outcrops and thickets of strawberry trees to a shoulder (370m). Not far downhill you reach a signpost and **farm road** (280m, **1hr 15min**).

Continue straight across the unsurfaced road and down past a paddock, keeping an eye out for faint paint splashes. These indicate a steepish descent beneath turkey oaks and cool undergrowth to the **Rivière de**

Vetricella (66m), which is easily forded thanks to large stepping stones. Over on the other side, turn L for an uphill track climbing out of the river valley to a **350m crest** (**1hr 20min**) and a clearing with huge juniper bushes, asphodels and a signpost. ▸

On a wider, older lane, you bear SSW between fields where livestock may be grazing. Waymarking then leads off for a path that concludes in the village of **Serriera** (80m, **40min**).

Small grocery store, drinking fountain and Mairie (Town Hall). A short stroll downhill is the former olive press, tastefully converted into the delightful *gîte d'étape* L'Alivi (tel 04 95104933 or 06 17559051, gite.etape.alivi@orange.fr, sleeps 32 in dorms and rooms, open Apr–Oct, accepts credit cards, no self-catering). Should you need it, 10min downhill on the main road is a bus stop for the Porto–Calvi service.

Visible just off the path are the photogenic abandoned stone houses of Pinedu.

Serriera has a marvellous mountainous backdrop

STAGE 7
Serriera to Ota

Start	Serriera
Distance	10.8km
Ascent	1050m
Descent	780m
Walking time	5hr 40min

After a lengthy taxing climb comes a memorable reward in the shape of brilliant views, a magnificent pine forest and a wild ravine down to a beautifully located hospitable village overlooking the Golfe de Porto.

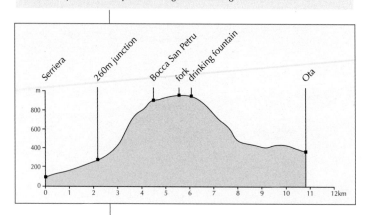

A little way uphill from the *gîte*, opposite the drinking fountain and shop in the village of Serriera (80m), follow orange markers down steps via the church and café to cross the river on a **footbridge**. You then join a wide dirt forestry track L climbing E for some 3km. At a **junction (260m)**, fork R on a clear path uphill into shady woodland. ◀ An outcrop overlooks Serriera and the surrounding wild hills, then the climb resumes amid pretty white blossoms of tree heather and scented lavender.

Circular clearings here were once used by charcoal burners.

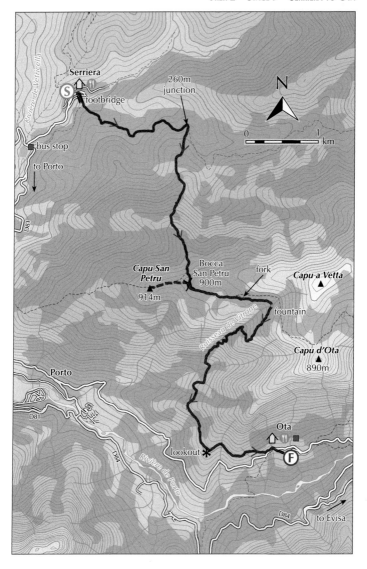

Majestic pines line the route in the forest near Capu San Petru

A fair way further up, the appearance of pines means you've almost completed the ascent to a broad crest clad in fresh green chestnut trees at **Bocca San Petru** (900m, 2hr 40min). Here, a recommended detour leads to a superb lookout, not to mention a perfect picnic spot.

Side trip to Capu San Petru (30min return)

Turn R for a clear level lane due W along the narrowing crest, thick with asphodels and bracken. As the lane starts to drop, go L through juniper shrubs and prepare to clamber the last easy metres to rock perches on **Capu San Petru** (914m), a breathtaking belvedere over the Golfe de Porto with views all the way from Capu Rossu to Scandola, and south across the valley to the eye-catching granite columns on Capu d'Ortu. Return the same way to **Bocca San Petru**.

Lookout points survey the coast, while closer at hand are massive rugged walls of deep red porphyry.

From Bocca San Petru, a wide path proceeds ESE, rising a little, as towering maritime pines alternate with sweet chestnut and even the rare peony. Some 15min on, keep your eyes peeled for a faint **fork** R, which you take. The path rounds the head of a valley and passes a drinking fountain before the long descent S commences, following the rugged Vitrone ravine. ◄ The stream is crossed several times, then followed closely in a series of knee-jarring steps dwarfed by oppressive cliffs.

Finally out of the ravine, the path swerves L past a little waterfall beneath a prominent rock point. Accompanied by hosts of orchids you gain a panoramic corner, then embark on the last leg due E with never-ending ups and downs as well as inspiring views inland, finally dropping to **Ota** (320m, 3hr).

Attractive Ota finally appears

Bus service to Porto, as well as food supplies and two popular *gîtes d'étape*: Chez Marie (tel 04 95261137, **www.gite-chez-marie.com**, sleeps 30 in rooms and dorms, open year-round, accepts credit cards) and Chez Félix (tel 06 72764956 or 04 9570649, **https://gitechezfelixota.com**, sleeps 50 in rooms and dorms, open year-round).

The pretty village of **Ota**, swarming with swifts, is well equipped for the multitude of walkers who flock here for the nearby Spilonca gorge. Draped in honeysuckle creepers and adorned with fragrant lime trees, it looks southwest to impressive Capu d'Ortu. In contrast, at the rear of the village, is modest Capu d'Ota, which looks like it's about to collapse and flatten the houses. However, the locals have no fears on this score as they believe it is anchored in place by three strong chains of a celestial nature.

STAGE 8

Ota to Marignana

Start	Ota
Distance	11.5km
Ascent	650m
Descent	260m
Walking time	4hr 50min

This is a beautiful landmark stage, negotiating the lovely Spilonca gorge crossed by elegant bridges. Do allow extra time for a swim and picnic. Once the route has climbed out to well-served Evisa with its al fresco cafés, you drop across a quiet river valley.

If it fits in with your plans, by all means leave the Mare e Monti at Evisa and head east over the mountains on the Mare a Mare Nord (slotting into Stage 3).

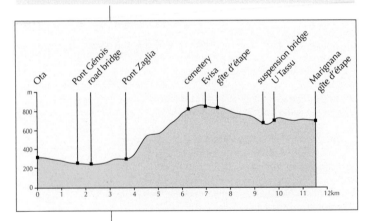

From the fountain at lovely Ota, head downhill past Chez Félix gîte d'étape to where a path takes over through terraced olive groves, gently descending to the Rivière de Porto. Orange markers lead along the rocky bank to

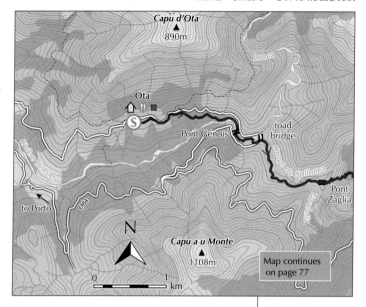

Map continues
on page 77

photogenic **Pont Génois** (200m, **40min**), spanning the river. ▶

Cross the bridge and follow the clear way as it continues L along the bank past a playing field and up to tarmac. Not far L is a **road bridge** at the confluence of the Lonca and the Aïtone. Here, fork R (signed for Spilonca) for the start of a delightful old mule track rambling up the right bank of the Aïtone amid bright masses of wildflowers. As you approach the Spilonca gorge, the rock walls become redder and more imposing, towering over walkers, and sections of path are cut into the cliffs. Flights of steps finally descend to another bridge, **Pont Zaglia** (280m, **40min**), over the Tavulella.

Dating back to 1797, **Pont Zaglia** was erected for shepherds and their livestock. Side paths lead off to water holes for swimming and relaxing, not a bad idea in view of the imminent stiff climb.

Also known as Ponte Vecchiu or Vechju (old bridge), this is reputedly the most beautiful restored 15th-century bridge of its kind on the island.

The path leads along the riverbank after the Pont Génois

Over the bridge, turn R (E). The gorge is soon left behind as you puff up tight switchbacks edged by old stone walls beneath evergreen oaks and pines. The path finally levels out as you reach the D84 at a **cemetery**. Here, turn L past Auberge La Châtaigneraie to a road fork. ◄ Keep straight on past a supermarket into the lovely scenic village of **Evisa** (850m, **2hr**).

If you don't need the village facilities, turn R at the fork for a shortcut via the *gîte d'étape* U Poghju.

Cafés and restaurants, tourist office (tel 04 95500687), bus to the coast and Ajaccio, accommodation including Hôtel Aïtone (tel 04 95262004, **www.hotel-aitone.com**). By all means take a day off and walk up to the renowned rock pools on the Aïtone.

Not far on, the Mare e Monti veers R past the post office for steps down to the road, where it's L to the family-run *gîte d'étape* U Poghju (tel 04 95262188 or 06 80838647, gite-etape-upoghju@orange.fr, sleeps 40, open Apr–mid Oct).

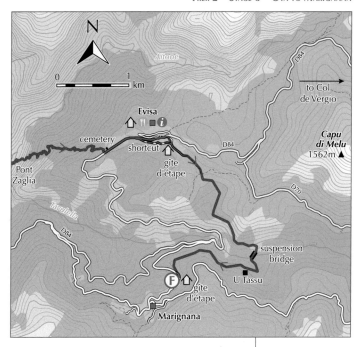

Proceed SE along the road. On a corner as the houses finish, branch off R for a descent via rough lanes to a stream crossing. Then follow an old wall before a steep drop to the Tavulella and a **suspension bridge** (635m, **40min**). The watercourse is crossed three more times, then a narrow path leads up to the abandoned hamlet of **U Tassu** (700m). A level stretch through chestnut woods brings you out at the road and **Marignana gîte d'étape** (700m, **50min**).

Gîte d'étape Ustaria di a Rota (tel 04 95262121, www.ustariadiarota.fr, sleeps 26 in rooms and dorms, always open, camping area). Groceries on sale. A further 10min up the road is Marignana village proper, with buses to Ajaccio.

STAGE 9

Marignana to E Case

Start	Marignana *gîte d'étape*
Distance	18km
Ascent	825m
Descent	930m
Walking time	6hr

This is an especially long day, entailing plenty of ups and downs and crossing wild rocky valleys, miles and marvellous miles from anywhere. Wildflowers feature high on the list of attractions. The stage concludes at a rustic walkers' hostel with an outlook to the coast.

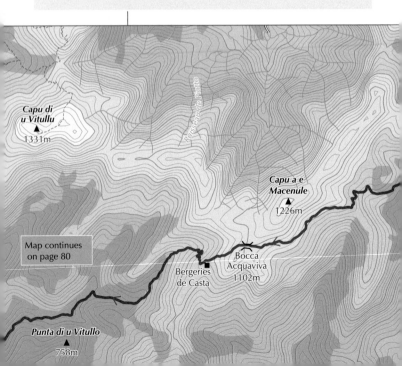

Capu di u Vitullu ▲ 1331m

Ruisseau de Fratu

Capu a e Macenule ▲ 1226m

Map continues on page 80

Bocca Acquaviva 1102m

Bergeries de Casta

Punta di u Vitullo ▲ 758m

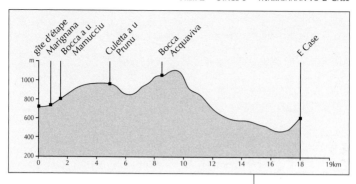

From the *gîte d'étape*, head up the road past the cemetery to Marignana (715m, **10min**). At the church, turn L up the cobbled streets to woodland teeming with foraging pigs. Past the playing ground is a cross at **Bocca a u Mamucciu** (824m, **30min**).

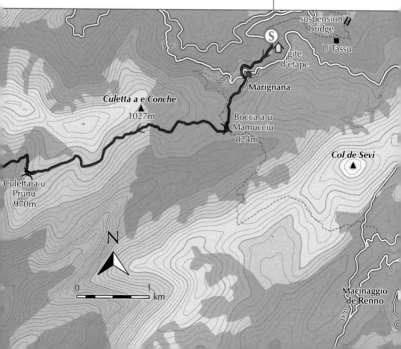

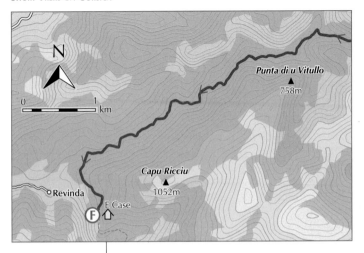

Some remarkably gnarled trees are encountered, testifying to their erstwhile importance to the local economy.

Turn sharp R onto a rough lane climbing to a crest, where you need to keep your eyes skinned for faint paint splashes marking the path L across rock slabs into a chestnut copse. Aromatic flowered maquis soon takes over and an old level mule track heads WSW with great views all the way to the coast. At a minor pass, **Culetta a u Prunu** (970m), the path narrows and turns decidedly R (N), descending into chestnut woods and past a *séchoir*, a type of hut once used for drying nuts. ◄

A couple of streams are crossed before you climb through a dramatic red cleft valley and resume a SW direction. Paved tracts of an old winding track appear from time to time, leading through a marvellous extended garden of rock roses, lilies and lavender, to name but a few. A gradual ascent across rougher scrubby terrain concludes at the ample panoramic saddle **Bocca Acquaviva** (1102m, **2hr 30min**), shaded by Capu a e Macenule.

Coasting W at first through overgrazed pasture past signs for a *source* (spring), you drop to the circular stone enclosures of the abandoned **Bergeries de Casta**. Follow cairns down the wide crest to an outcrop at 960m, where tight zigzags plunge into the densely wooded valley of

The old way negotiates stark rock gullies on the way to E Case

Riogna with its many streams. A long, easy wander SW through shady woodland of strawberry trees and evergreen oak leads past a signed fork (R) for the hamlet of **Revinda**. A short way further on (SE) you reach the isolated *gîte d'étape* of **E Case** (605m, **2hr 50min**), wonderfully situated overlooking the coast and Golfe de Chiuni.

> *Gîte d'étape* E Case (tel 04 95264819 or 06 82499565, sleeps 19, open Apr–Oct) is a simple family-run stone farmhouse, extending a warm welcome to weary walkers. Meals are served al fresco and supplies come in courtesy of the mule. Don't expect any mod cons though.

STAGE 10
E Case to Cargèse

Start	E Case
Distance	13km
Ascent	400m
Descent	910m
Walking time	4hr 30min

This is a straightforward, if not exceptionally exciting, concluding stage of a wonderful long-distance experience. The destination Cargèse (or Carghjese) is a good place to collapse as it has a full range of creature comforts and the added attraction of beaches!

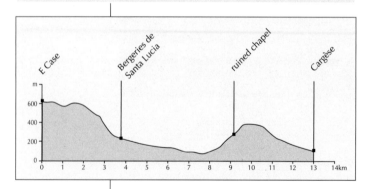

There are views back to Revinda, as well as to the promising coast ahead.

Head off SE into shoulder-high maquis across a gurgling stream and continue in gradual ascent through lilies galore, then gigantic strawberry trees, to the rocky crests of **Pianu Maggiore**, culminating at 650m. ◄

After an outcrop (471m), turn sharp L following a fence for a scrambly drop through dry scrub alongside paddocks. This finally terminates at a dirt track at

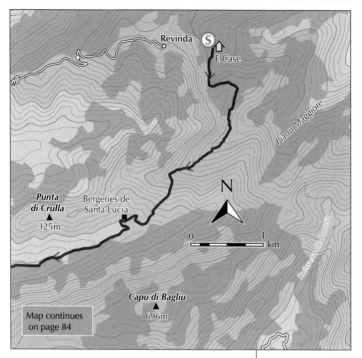

Bergeries de Santa Lucia (220m, **1hr 40min**). Follow the
lane that loops down past a fork to cross the Esigna river
(190m) and stay on it for a matter of kilometres W. After
a succession of crossings, you reach a junction for Lozzi,
but fork L to ford the watercourse (70m).

Waymarking needs following carefully for the ensuing climb along a series of lanes and sunken paths overgrown with brambles and stinging nettles. You emerge
at a cluster of farms on a road close to a **ruined chapel**
(380m, **2hr**) in Romanesque style. The route turns W
enclosed by old stone walls through farmland, eventually
dropping through scrub to a road. Go L then first R for the
little-used D181, and down to the crossroads of **Cargèse**
(96m, **50min**). ▸

The population of
Cargèse is of Greek
origin, thanks to the
16th-century refugees
who fled here from
persecution under
the Ottoman Empire.

83

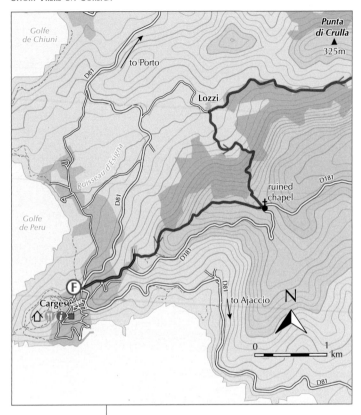

The sun-soaked town of Cargèse offers all supplies and services, including ATM and buses to Ajaccio and Calvi. Tourist office (tel 04 95264131). Hôtel Punta e Mare (tel 04 95264433 or 06 89724181, **www.locations-cargese.com**) and Hôtel Saint Jean (tel 04 95264668, www.lesaintjean.com). Treat yourself to a swim at Plage de Peru, a splendid sandy beach a 15min stagger down the hill. Nearby is Hôtel Ta Kladia (tel 04 95264073, **www.motel-takladia.com**).

TREK 3

Mare a Mare Nord: Cargèse to Moriani Plage

Start	Cargèse
Finish	Moriani Plage
Distance	148.2km
Walking time	11 days
Maps	IGN 1:25,000, sheets 4151OT, 4150OT, 4250OT, 4351OT
Access	Year-round buses connect Cargèse to Ajaccio, as well as to Porto and Ota. Transport points along the way that are handy for exit/entry include Evisa (year-round bus to Ajaccio), Col de Vergio, Albertacce and Calacuccia (summer bus to Corte), and Corte which is on the Bastia–Ajaccio train line. Moriani Plage, the trek's conclusion, has year-round bus links with Bastia and Porto-Vecchio.

Also referred to as the Traversale Nord, this highly recommended, strenuous coast-to-coast route takes you through the heart of Corsica. Beginning on the stunning west coast, it heads inland via spectacular river gorges and high mountain passes before reaching the island's ancient political and cultural centre, Corte. The concluding days meander through quiet hilltop villages before descending to the lovely eastern seaboard looking over to Tuscany.

Waymarking is orange paint stripes. There are several lengthy stages, but also plenty of alternatives and exit/entry points. Fit walkers could compress a couple of stages and complete the trek in eight to nine days if desired. On the other hand, it's fun allowing for days out to explore beauty spots – for example Col de Vergio and Corte.

For the first two and a half days as far as Evisa, the Mare a Mare Nord (MMN) is in common with the popular Mare e Monti trek, meaning that accommodation is shared, so book ahead to avoid disappointment.

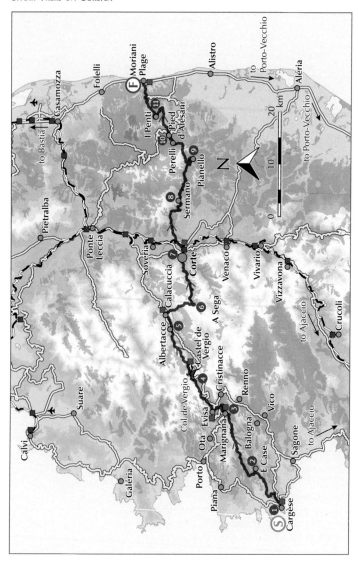

CARGÈSE

The route start, laid-back Cargèse, is known as the 'town of the Greeks' due to 16th-century refugees from the Ottoman Empire, and boasts its own Orthodox church as well as a handful of Greek-speaking inhabitants. On the practical side, it has full visitor facilities, ATM, lovely beaches and a choice of accommodation such as Hôtel Punta e Mare (tel 04 95264433 or 06 89724181, www.locations-cargese.com) and Hôtel Saint Jean (tel 04 95264668, www.lesaintjean.com). Tourist office (tel 04 95264131).

STAGE 1
Cargèse to E Case

Start	Cargèse
Distance	13km
Ascent	910m
Descent	400m
Walking time	5hr

The opening section of this great traverse consists of alternating steady climbs and brief descents. The culmination is a simple but memorable *gîte d'étape*.

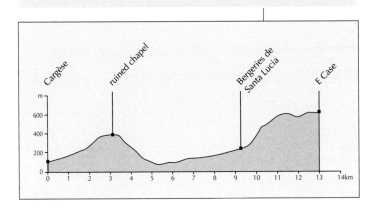

There are lovely views to the beaches and one of the island's ubiquitous Genoese watchtowers, along with far-off Capu Rossu.

At the crossroads and monument overlooking the sea at Cargèse (96m), take the D181 road NE past a supermarket, signed for the Mare e Monti trek. Some 10min up, as the coast comes into view S, fork L to where a marked path sets out through low scrub. ◄ You climb steadily through rural properties via a series of gates to a broad crest, before touching on a road and farms at a **ruined chapel** (380m, **1hr 15min**) of Romanesque design.

Following signs for Lozzi, turn sharp L (N) down a shady path which reverts to an overgrown sunken lane. This eventually joins a broad track leading to a stream ford (70m), where you go R (bypassing the hamlet of **Lozzi**). Beneath old olive trees, following the Esigna

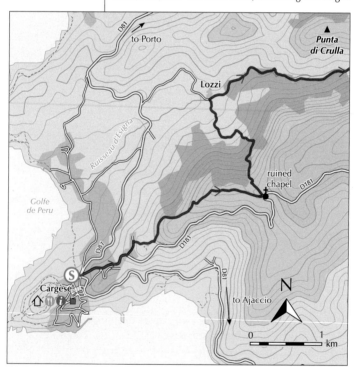

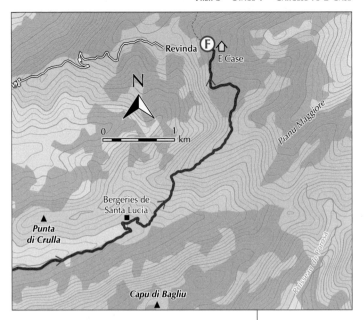

watercourse and crossing back and forth in a heavily
wooded valley topped by pink rock ridges, the track
heads essentially E in imperceptible ascent for several kilometres. At around 190m, it crosses over to the left bank
to loop up to the huddle of shepherds' huts **Bergeries de
Santa Lucia** (220m, **1hr 45min**).

From here, a narrow path takes over for the steep
scrambly haul NE up through dry maquis. You follow a
wire fence to gain a ridge (471m). A series of rock outcrops punctuate the lovely **Pianu Maggiore** crest, bright
with rock roses and broom. ▸ A little more ascent is
needed (to 650m), then it levels out through a wood of
huge strawberry trees. A shady descent with masses of
Corsican lilies leads to a stream crossing, handy for cooling feet. The concluding stretch NW climbs briefly to a
clearing and the isolated and remarkably scenic position
of the *gîte d'étape* **E Case** (605m, **2hr**).

Views range across
the rolling wooded
hills and take in the
hamlet of Revinda,
as well as the coast.

*The gîte d'étape
E Case at the
conclusion of Stage 1*

Overlooking the splendid Golfe de Chiuni, this converted stone farmhouse with basic facilities extends a lovely welcome to walkers (tel 04 95264819 or 06 82499565, sleeps 19, open Apr–Oct). Meals are served al fresco and supplies are brought in from the nearby roadhead at Revinda.

STAGE 2

E Case to Marignana

Start	E Case
Distance	18km
Ascent	930m
Descent	825m
Walking time	6hr

A very long stage, but particularly splendid and rewarding with extended wild stretches, glorious views and masses of wildflowers. Some walkers may prefer to press on to Evisa for hotel accommodation – a further 1hr 30min. But be warned, that makes an even longer haul and entails steepish downs and ups.

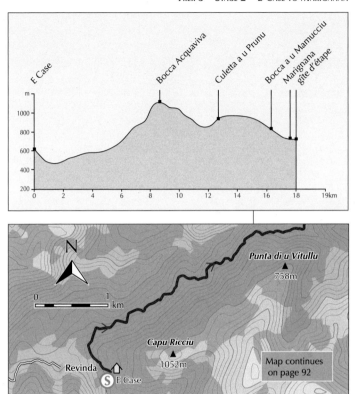

Take the clear path through shoulder-high maquis, ignoring the turn-off L for **Revinda** a short way along. Proceeding NE in shady woods, you follow the thickly wooded valley of Riogna for a while, crossing countless streams before zigzagging decidedly uphill to a pano-ramic outcrop (960m) spread with lavender, juniper and asphodels. Marked by cairns, the faint path soon reaches a series of circular stone enclosures (**Bergeries de Casta**) amid scented broom. Past signs for a *source* (spring), pro-ceed above abandoned pasture to the distinct saddle of **Bocca Acquaviva** (1102m, **3hr**). ▶

Set at the foot of modest Capu a e Macenule, the saddle offers vast views to distant inland mountains.

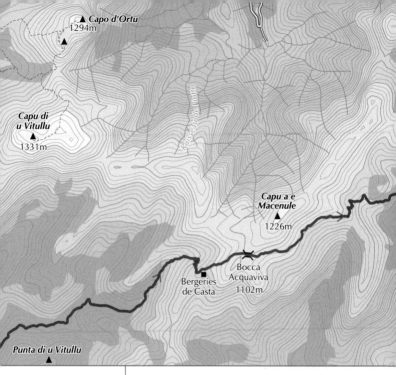

Maintaining the same direction, the route negotiates rougher loose stony terrain, threading its way through scratchy bushes in gradual diagonal descent. You will find an absolutely glorious range of splendid flowers in this beautiful wild area, miles from roads. Vestiges of the original mule track appear, leading you into a dramatic red cleft valley.

A couple of stream crossings precede yet another climb – this time via remarkable chestnut woods with ancient knobbly trees and welcome fresh green foliage. Past a ruined stone hut that once served as a *séchoir* for drying nuts, the path winds up to the minor pass **Culetta a u Prunu** (970m) on an open scenic ridge.

Bearing ENE, the old mule track coasts through more crazily flowered slopes and across rock slabs, with views all the way down to Corsica's west coast. A chestnut

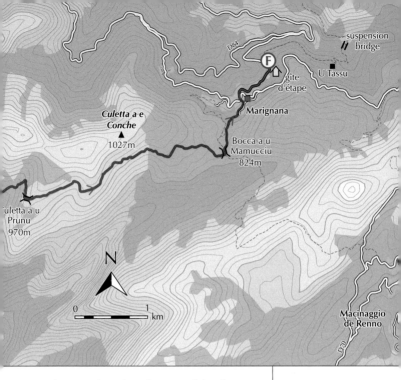

copse is traversed to a rise, where a rough lane is encountered and you turn R in stumbling descent to the cross at **Bocca a u Mamucciu** (824m, **2hr 30min**), where a MMN variant breaks off SE (ignore it).

Turn L alongside a football field amid pigs, foraging and lazing. Not far on are views to dramatic river gorges as the path quickly descends through the cobbled streets and modest stone dwellings of quiet **Marignana** (715m, **20min**, year-round bus to Ajaccio). When you reach the church, turn R along the road and past the cemetery for the **gîte d'étape** (700m, **10min**).

Gîte d'étape Ustaria di a Rota (tel 04 95262121, **www.ustariadiarota.fr**, sleeps 26 in rooms and dorms, always open, camping area). Groceries on sale.

STAGE 3
Marignana to Castel de Vergio

Start	Marignana
Distance	15.8km
Ascent	880m
Descent	120m
Walking time	5hr 30min

After the attractive village of Evisa (with shops and hotels), this marvellous day takes in the magnificent Aïtone forest of towering Corsican pines, run through by a beautiful succession of cascades and attractive rock pools, not to mention photogenic suspension bridges. There are plenty of opportunities here for taking time out. The walk concludes near a medium-altitude pass amid exciting alpine scenery.

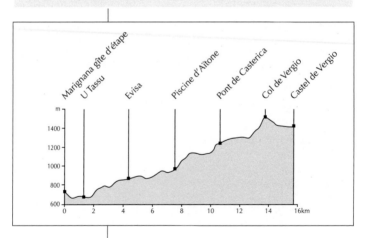

From the *gîte*, take the path parallel to the road through chestnut woods for a gradual descent into a side valley to the evocative abandoned settlement of **U Tassu** (700m), which is worth exploring. You then drop steeply to a stream

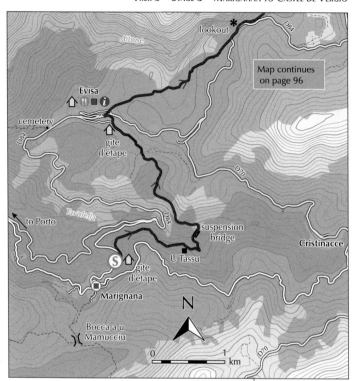

to cross it three times in quick succession, before traversing the Tavulella on a **suspension bridge** (635m, **30min**).

The ensuing steep ascent through Mediterranean oak and maquis includes several lookout points over the tortuous road and gorge, then a gentler stretch along an old wall in shady woods. After a stream crossing, rough vehicle tracks lead up to a road. Turn L for the nearby family-run *gîte d'étape* U Poghju on the lower reaches of Evisa (tel 04 95262188 or 06 80838647, gite-etape-upoghju@orange.fr, sleeps 40, open Apr–mid Oct). Not far along the road, take the flight of steps to the upper part of the village of **Evisa** (850m, **1hr**).

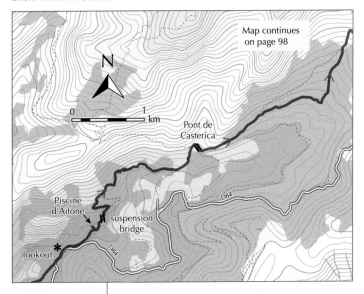

Grocery shops, cafés and restaurants, tourist office (tel 04 95500687), year-round bus to Ajaccio and the coast, and a handful of hotels including Hôtel Aïtone (tel 04 95262004, **www.hotel-aitone.com**).

On the main road opposite the steps you came up, you need the Chemin des Châtaigniers (Chestnut Way), lined with info boards about chestnut harvesting and drying, once a principal activity in this region. It climbs via a concrete ramp to a MMN signpost. Take the delightful lane E past pig sheds and hosts of magnificent ancient chestnut trees. A muddy stretch between old stone walls leads uphill to a car park, where you briefly join the road. ◀ Then a broad lane lined with foxgloves and lofty pines continues on to a fork. Here, keep L for the time being, descending high rock steps for the nearby **Piscine d'Aïtone** (910m, **1hr**), a magnificent series of cascades and huge deep green pools shaded by the forest – a popular spot for family picnics and bathing. ◀

Don't miss the path L for a quick there-and-back diversion to a superb lookout high above the Aïtone river.

Take care as the rocks can be slippery.

Retrace your steps back up to the top; but a tad before the fork, **turn L** (NE) across a side stream and follow the pretty bank to a **suspension bridge**, which leads to a steep ascent through stunning pine forest. Higher up is a scramble over rock slabs colonised by bright broom shrubs. The ensuing gentle descent through fresh green beech trees approaches the Aïtone once again, past an unusable bridge hanging in threads. Walk on uphill through a delightful forest of fir trees, holly and masses of tree heather to join a concrete-based forestry track R to nearby **Pont de Casterica** (1186m, **1hr 10min**) and more superb rock pools.

Just across the bridge, **turn L** and follow a clear, mostly level track through beech woods for around half an hour before an abrupt **turn L**. A steep slog follows a stony stream bed, where encounters with roaming pigs are common. The woods eventually thin out, giving way to magnificent Corsican pines, accompanied by hellebore, asphodels and bracken. You finally reach the road pass **Col de Vergio** (1478m, **1hr 15min**), popular with coach tours (kiosk with snacks and souvenirs, summer bus to Corte).

Col de Vergio and its curious statue

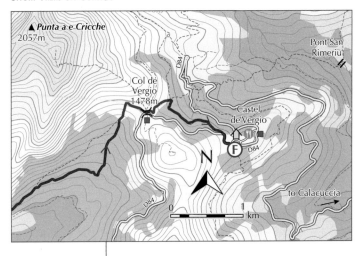

The watershed at **Col de Vergio** (or Col de Verghio) affords sweeping views down to the Calacuccia dam in the Niolo district. It also has an impressive gigantic stone statue of Christ Roi atop a structure reminiscent of an igloo.

From the opposite side of the car park, take the path marked with yellow paint stripes, dropping E. A mere 10min downhill you encounter the broad GR20, which you join for the short final section of the stage – turn R following red/white markers. ◄ A gentle uphill leads out to the roadside close to the winter skiing area at **Hôtel Castel de Vergio** (1400m, **35min**).

En route are extraordinary examples of Corsican pines and silver birch.

This cavernous, congenial establishment – the highest hotel in Corsica – caters for long-distance walkers with big appetites; it's worth taking a day out here to rest or explore the surrounds (tel 04 95480001, **www.hotel-castel-vergio.com**, sleeps 130 in modern rooms and cabin dormitories, accepts credit cards, camping ground, groceries). Summer bus to Corte.

STAGE 4
Castel de Vergio to Albertacce

Start	Castel de Vergio
Distance	13.4km
Ascent	160m
Descent	700m
Walking time	4hr

Today's route passes into the central uplands of the Niolo district through more forest, with rivers and a picturesque Genoese bridge. Crowned by the island's highest peaks, the region was long renowned for harbouring bandits. It maintains its traditions of raising livestock and producing memorable ewe's milk cheeses.

At day's end, instead of overnighting at tiny Albertacce, those needful of a wider range of facilities can proceed to the next village, Calacuccia (1hr away – see Stage 5).

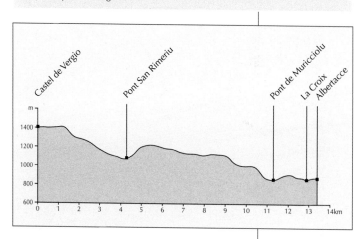

From Hôtel Castel de Vergio, backtrack briefly up the road to where the red/white waymarked GR20 breaks off R (NW). Follow it past attractive stands of silver birch

The veritable maze of forestry tracks means you need to keep a constant eye out for waymarks.

The old bridge affords lovely views NNW to triangular Punta Licciola.

and majestic Corsican pines to the intersection encountered in Stage 3. Here, turn sharp R (E) on the MMN, with yellow markings for the time being. After a gradual descent in tall pine forest, it crosses the road twice and passes a military zone. ◄

About an hour downhill, you reach a pretty cascading side stream with lovely pools, then the mighty Golo river, which has descended a fair way from where it rises at the foot of the Paglia Orba. A level track leads E to **Pont San Rimeriu** (1049m, **1hr 20min**). ◄

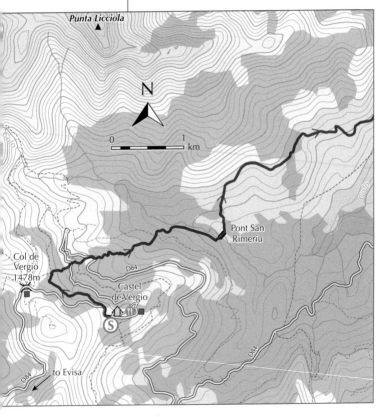

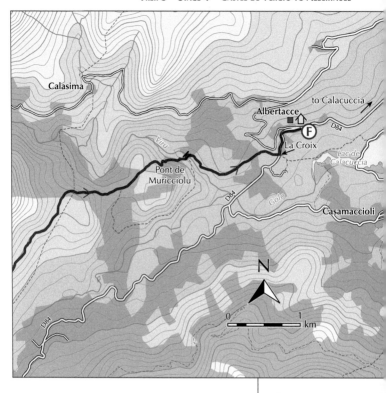

On the opposite bank, climb straight ahead past a couple of huts (Bergerie de Tillerga) into mixed woods thick with lilies. The pleasant and clearly signed path moves NE down the left side of the partially wooded valley, at times crossing open moorland populated by ferns, asphodels, broom and pungent herbs. ▶ Further down is a path fork (which you ignore) and great mountain views: first and foremost, due north, is Corsica's highest peak, Monte Cintu (2706m), spattered with snow in spring, while closer are the Cinque Frati (Five Friars), north-northwest. A flat stretch traverses shady chestnut woods then drops to **Pont de Muricciolu** (835m, **2hr**).

Attractive wind-sculptured rock formations dot the way.

The marvellous arch of Pont de Muricciolu

Pont de Muricciolu turns out to be a photogenic humpback bridge over the Viru river, and an old mill, not to mention a wonderful picnic and bathing spot. Exciting views take in Paglia Orba and Capu Tafunatu.

Head E past a shrine and over an impressive gorge where the River Viru flows into the Golo. Small-scale farms start to appear, and not far downhill is a road and prominent cross **La Croix** marking the southern entrance to the quiet village. ◄ A short distance L is **Albertacce** (854m, **40min**).

If you don't intend to visit Albertacce, go straight ahead for Calacuccia.

Albertacce has a modest museum of local archae-ological finds as well as a well-reputed *gîte d'étape* (tel 04 95480560 or 06 17266706, sleeps 20, open Apr–Sept). The Corte–Col de Vergio bus passes this way.

STAGE 5

Albertacce to A Sega

Start	Albertacce
Distance	12.6km
Ascent	800m
Descent	450m
Walking time	5hr 15min

Climbing out of the Niolo district, this exhilarating section incorporates the route's highest pass (1592m), which ushers you into the magnificent wild Tavignano valley. A lengthy ascent is involved, so try to set out early as it can be hot going in the noon sun.

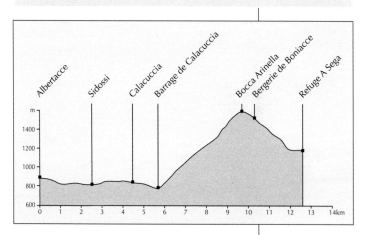

Return to **La Croix** and the signed junction to pick up the trail, turning L (E) across scrubby overgrazed land to the edge of Lake Calacuccia. Beneath chestnut trees, a succession of dusty lanes shared with foraging pigs lead to the road, D218.

Turn L into nearby sleepy **Sidossi** (800m), which boasts a café, restaurant and church. Not far on, after

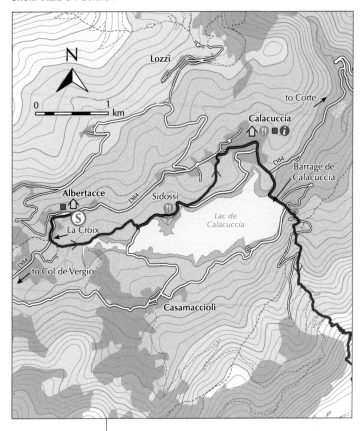

the bend, you need the signed old mule track L (NE) that climbs gently to a cemetery, which you skirt L to reach the main road D84. Go R past the church for **Calacuccia** (812m, **1hr**).

ATM, cafés, restaurants, shops, year-round bus to Corte. Tourist office (04 95471262). Lovely old-style rose-smothered Hôtel des Touristes, which doubles as the *gîte* (tel 04 95480004, www.hotel-des-touristes-corse.fr, open May–Oct, no cooking facilities). Otherwise 10min W out of town is Hôtel Acqua Viva (tel 04 95480690).

Head S towards the lake again, turning R at the crossroads for the dam, **Barrage de Calacuccia** (794m, **30min**). ▸ At the far end of the wall, a marked path heads essentially S, confused at times with sheep tracks. Ascending steadily amid scrubby vegetation, it short-cuts the wide curves of a dirt track, passing the modest abodes of herders. Further up, the easy zigzags of an ancient mule track are followed, taking the sting out of what would otherwise be a steep climb. Passing across windswept land populated by grazing herds of cows and sheep, you finally gain the broad open crest and fence marking **Bocca Arinella** (1592m, **2hr 30min**).

Constructed in 1968 to provide Bastia with a reliable water supply, the dam created Lake Calacuccia, whose surface reflects the marvellous rugged mountains rising beyond the broad Niolo valley.

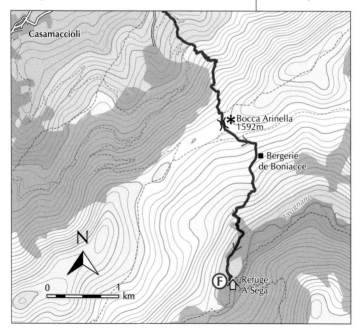

From **Bocca Arinella** there's an amazing panorama of mountains and valleys any way you look! Magnificent red kites can often be seen surveying the ridge for a meal.

A marked track leads off SE to cross a lane and pass a cluster of huts, **Bergerie de Boniacce** (1500m). The descent S now begins in earnest towards the very promising wild wooded valley at your feet. Remarkable concentrations of the showy white Corsican lily accompany the path until it reaches conifer woods, which gradually gather force and provide welcome shade as you zigzag down towards the river. A final stretch R takes you through to **Refuge A Sega** (1190m, **1hr 15min**).

Reservations at **www.pnr.corsica**. Tel 09 72661987, sleeps 36, open May–Oct, self-catering, camping. Spacious modern construction stunningly placed on the banks of the Tavignano river, with marvellous if chilly rock pools close at hand. It extends a warm welcome to walkers and serves tasty homemade fare. Supplies are brought in on horseback or by helicopter.

Refuge A Sega

STAGE 6

A Sega to Corte

Start	A Sega
Distance	13.3km
Ascent	100m
Descent	770m
Walking time	4hr 15min

This entire day is spent in the magnificent Tavignano river valley cloaked with a memorable forest of towering Corsican pines. The valley narrows to a marvellous deep gorge in the middle section. Historic inspiration for today's stage can be drawn from the widely held belief that this was the route taken by Napoleon's parents, fleeing from Corte and the victorious French army over to the west coast since they opposed the new French rulers (who had recently purchased Corsica) as well as the former Genoese rulers. They travelled by mule, his mother well advanced in her expectant state with the great man.

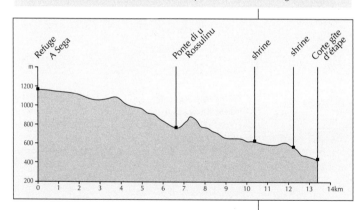

A stone's throw from Refuge A Sega, a timber bridge affords a wonderful view of the brilliant green waters of the Tavignano cascading through rock pools. ▶ On the opposite bank you pass the decrepit hut and former refuge...consider yourself lucky you didn't have to spend the night there!

The pale granite banks are coloured delicate hues courtesy of rainbow lichens and splashes of broom.

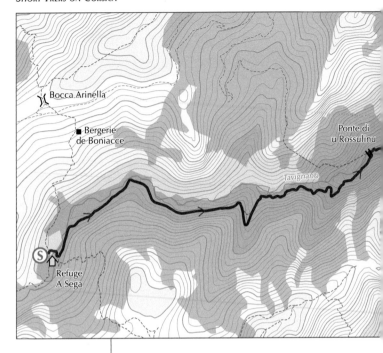

This former mule track is an incredible feat of engineering, with surprisingly long stretches still intact thanks to stone reinforcing and paving.

Cruising easily NE initially, the MMN follows the course of the river closely at first, but as the mountainside becomes steeper, the path cuts a safe if narrow passage between charred pine trees, dizzily high above the crashing river in sheer-sided ravines. ◄ It's a matter of continual ups and downs, the route weaving its way between crazy rock points with giddy views. Several side streams are crossed, and only at the last moment does the track make up its mind to actually descend in earnest to the level of the watercourse and the long-awaited bridge **Ponte di u Rossulinu** (760m, **2hr**), a lovely spot to cool off.

The route crosses the bridge to find a dramatically different atmosphere on the opposite bank of the Tavignano. The pine forest disappears abruptly, and this is soon the realm of drier maquis shrubs such as tree

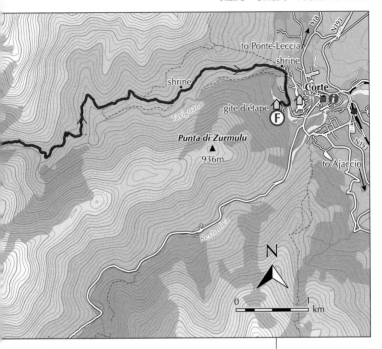

heather, Mediterranean oak and the colourful scented blooms of broom and lavender.

Wider and regularly paved, the path proceeds essentially E, the low vegetation allowing views of totem-pole-like rock needles, as well as the plunging river bed below. The township of Corte is soon glimpsed, and more side streams and pools encountered. A dense mass of white rock rose is traversed, followed by maritime pines with red fissured bark. A **shrine** with picnic tables precedes abandoned terracing before the final ups and downs past a second **shrine** to a road at the rear of the citadel on the outskirts of **Corte**, aka Corti (420m). ▸ For the *gîte*, turn R in descent, then R again across the now placid Tavignano. After a car park, a lane winds up to the peaceful shady spot of **gîte d'étape** U Tavignanu (**2hr 15min**).

Turn L down Rue St-Joseph for the town centre and hotels (10min).

109

Gîte d'étape U Tavignanu is a laid-back family-run establishment with excellent meals (tel 04 95461685 or 06 86902386, gite.utavignanu@ orange.fr, sleeps 20, open year-round, no self-catering). Camping ground.

Corte has ATM, shops, restaurants and hotels such as Hôtel de la Paix (tel 04 95460672, http:// hoteldelapaix-corte.fr). Tourist office (tel 04 95462670). Trains to Ajaccio, Bastia and Calvi as well as buses in most directions.

Corte is a great place to enjoy a day off – visit the charming historic town with its steep cobbled streets, teetering houses, fountains and belvedere citadel; listen to traditional men's chanting/singing; and stock up on groceries, as no shops are encountered on the final five days of the MMN until Moriani Plage, at the very end.

Corte's old citadel

STAGE 7

Corte to Sermano

Start	Corte
Distance	16km
Ascent	1000m
Descent	700m
Walking time	5hr 40min

The excitement of Corte behind you, this stage gets away from it all traversing the quiet rural district of Boziu dotted with scenically placed villages. While landscapes tend to be barer than the past few days, in compensation they swarm with roaming livestock, and magnificent birds of prey are a common sight. A number of abrupt climbs and subsequent drops make the long day rather tiring.

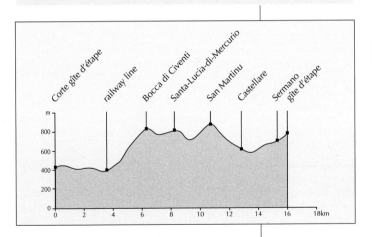

From the *gîte*, retrace your steps back up to the rear of the citadel of Corte and yesterday's junction. The MMN now takes Rue St-Joseph R in descent to a crossroads where you go L then almost immediately R down to cross Boulevard Paoli (facing Hôtel du Nord). ▶ Take

If you stayed in town, join the route here.

Avenue Jean Nicoli downhill past a car park and university premises to the river and a major intersection. Now, straight ahead, you need the quiet road D39.

A mere 5min along, you are pointed off L (at Résidence Goria) and soon find yourself in green fields and gently rolling hills populated by herds of sheep grazing amid rock rose shrubs. After a stream crossing (the Bistugliu) on stepping stones, a messy sunken way leads up to the single-track **railway line** where you need the pedestrian tunnel. There are lovely views back over Corte to snow-specked mountains, although these improve notably during the climb ahead.

The way bears diagonally L in steady ascent on well-marked paths across over-grazed hillsides crammed with cistus and ferns, culminating at the ample saddle **Bocca di Civenti** (785m, **1hr 40min**). ◄ The clear path proceeds E, cutting across a flank thick with marvellous aromatic maquis herbs before negotiating steep paved alleys to the scenic square of **Santa-Lucia-di-Mercurio** (820m, **50min**),

Here, panoramas include prominent Monte Rotondo southwest over the Restonica valley, with its overlapping waves of ridges.

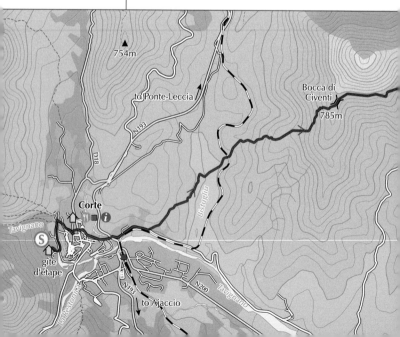

a pretty, well-kept village with sweeping views, drinking water and chambre d'hôtes (tel 06 88980292).

Walk past the cenotaph to a roadside cross where a concreted lane branches down R – but take the narrow path sharp L. Moving off E in the company of honeysuckle and dog roses, you drop via a succession of hamlets to a road then embark on two stream crossings before reaching a modest valley with a trickling stream. Chestnut trees make their appearance, then shady Mediterranean oak takes over. You climb to cross a road and quickly emerge on a high ridge at the scenically located chapel of **San Martinu** (904m, **1hr**).

Faint at first, a series of tight zigzags descend S down the hillside, enlivened by bushes of woolly yellow button flowers along with noisy jays and wood pigeons. You coast through elderberry and poppies via ancient stone walls and a fountain, before entering quiet **Castellare** (610m, **40min**, drinking fountain in main square). Walk down the road past the Mairie (Town Hall) for a short stretch N and

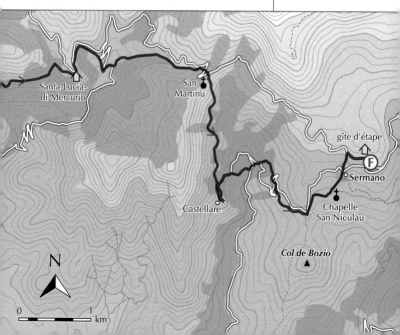

Sermano looks over to Monte Cardo

Monte d'Oro with its trademark knobbly point is clearly recognisable southwest, while much closer at hand (east) is Col de Bozio.

break off R just after the cemetery to embark on a shady sunken way NE to a stream crossing (565m).

As usual, any descent is followed by a stiff climb, cutting across the D41 several times. As the woods come to an end, hillside pastures take over. ◄ After a path junction (Mare a Mare variant for Poggio Venaco), you bear L (NE) on a level for the last leg, with the village of Sermano now visible not too far ahead. After the final stream crossing for the day, a ramp leads past 12th-century **Chapelle San Niculau** and the cemetery, up past tomorrow's fork for Alando, and steeply up into the pretty village of **Sermano** or Sermanu (750m, **1hr 15min**). From the main road, you're pointed up past the church for the day's final slog to the **gîte d'étape** (**15min**).

Gîte U San Fiurenzu (tel 06 13178494, usanfiurenzu@gmail.com, sleeps 12, open Apr–Oct, accepts credit cards, no kitchen facilities). Comfortable place with a lovely terrace for drying your laundry or enjoying a well-earned beer in contemplation of twin-peaked Monte Cardo looming southwest.

STAGE 8
Sermano to Pianello

Start	Sermano
Distance	13km
Ascent	650m
Descent	650m
Walking time	4hr 45min
Note	The stage is peppered with stream fords, several of which require extra care due to fallen trees and minor landslips.

Another tiring but rewarding day that leads up and down hill and dale, dropping in on beautifully placed picturesque hamlets resting on wooded mountain flanks, their slate roofs red and grey. You traverse a long wild ridge that culminates at a lovely village and well-run *gîte d'étape*. Vast panoramas are the flavour of the day, both inland and to the distant east coast at last.

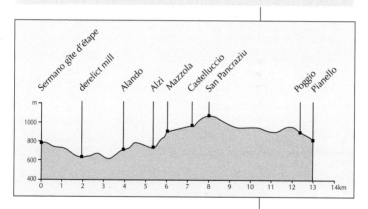

From the *gîte*, return to Sermano (750m) and take the orange-marked route past the post office and downhill past a huddle of ruined stone houses to yesterday's fork to Alando; turn L. The stony way passes a solar farm akin to a giant electronic tablet and proceeds on a scenic ramble accompanied by dog roses. Down in a wooded valley is

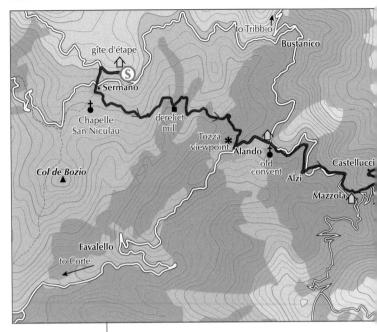

the first of four stream crossings on this opening stretch. After a **derelict mill** (615m), a ghostly corridor of blackened tree trunks winds E to the final crossing – watch your step as the path has collapsed in places. You climb out to the road at **Alando**, aka Alundu (710m, **1hr 30min**, drinking fountain).

At Alando there is a recommended signposted 10min-return detour to the adjacent knoll of **Tozza**, where a brilliant belvedere and enamelled *table d'orientation* show all the landmarks for 360 degrees.

Turn L along the road, via a monument for a 14th-century patriot, to a rambling old **convent** (opposite is chambre d'hôtes Couvent d'Alando, tel 04 95486421 or 06 38495349). Keep R on the D339. Not far along is

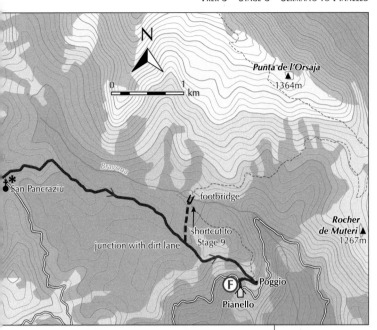

One of the stream crossings on the way to Alando

By all means ignore this and stick with the road to Alzi.

an easy-to-miss fork sharp R on a messy path dropping briefly SE to a stream, then a lane through chestnut trees to **Alzi** (780m). ◄

Here, the MMN takes a path just above the road, which is rejoined further along. Soon you're forked steeply up to **Mazzola** (900m) (accommodation at Casa di Lucia B&B, tel 04 9359084). Immediately before the church, take the gated steps uphill past houses onto a clear path heading up NE through woods. This cuts across tarmac before joining a narrow road L for spectacularly located **Castelluccio** (975m), comprising a handful of traditional houses, cherry trees and a cool well with built-in benches – a perfect picnic spot, where you can see all the way back to Sermano.

This point marks the trail's farewell to the mountainous interior, as you get promising glimpses of the sea and begin to breathe in its scent.

A short but steady ascent through chestnut woods thick with ferns emerges on an outcrop known as **San Pancraziu** (1020m, **1hr 30min**), an unpretentious chapel with a marvellous outlook, drinking water and a picnic table. ◄

The level route E leads to delightful fresh green beech woods as you follow a crest high above pasture land. Later on, the terrain opens out to maquis cover of tree heather and asphodels, inhabited by cuckoos and chaotic wood pigeons, and with a good chance of birds of prey.

To bypass Pianello, turn L at the dirt lane and slot into Stage 9 at the footbridge over the Bravona canyon.

You dip across a **dirt lane** and down to splash over a stream. ◄ A sunken way climbs up to a ridge and lane, where you now have a wonderful view over villages strung out below, all the way down to the coastal plain and the glittering sea. A clear path across sparkling rock slabs through masses of white lilies leads to the road then the houses of **Poggio** – and the junction with tomorrow's route. Follow waymarks and your instinct down the linking lanes heading for the prominent church of **Pianello** (803m, **1hr 45min**).

Opposite the church is the refurbished former school, now a friendly council-owned *gîte* with top catering, looking out over the coastal plain to the sea (tel 06 08094433, a.casapieri2b@gmail.com, sleeps 18, open Apr–Oct).

STAGE 9

Pianello to Pied d'Alesani

Start	Pianello
Distance	13km
Ascent	600m
Descent	750m
Walking time	4hr 15min

This region is known as the Castagniccia for its bountiful chestnuts and the inhabitants' traditional reliance on the tree for their livelihood. Remarkably ancient exemplars can be admired en route today, and there's a 1000+year-old tree near Pianello. Long wild stretches across uplands alternate with farming villages. Enticing views to the coast become a constant companion.

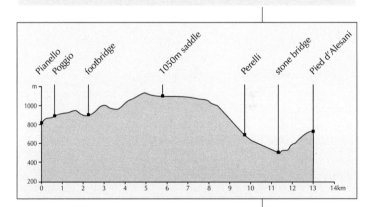

From the *gîte* at Pianello, retrace your steps up to the signed junction that you passed yesterday at **Poggio**. Head up past the old village oven and onto a mostly level way NW through chestnut trees for a minor stream crossing. Not far along is a **footbridge** (**45min**) over the Bravona where it cascades through an exciting canyon. ▶

The path climbs out to pick up an absolutely delightful old way ENE traversing open moorland with heather,

Yesterday's shortcut bypassing Pianello rejoins the route here.

119

clumps of hellebore and wild mint, in contrast to the bright green swathes of beech and rocky Punto de l'Orsaja above. A stream crossing is followed by a short climb past giant fire-blackened chestnut trees before the traverse resumes contouring around the 1000m mark in the company of scented broom. At a **saddle** (1050m, **1hr 45min**), thick with bracken and dug up ruinously by boars, you veer L (N) on a rougher path threading its way down past spectacularly giant chestnut trees. A water tank marks your arrival at a road. Continue in the same direction down a

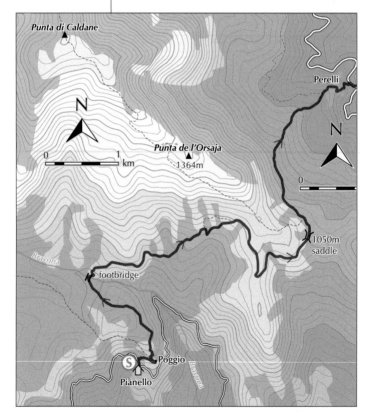

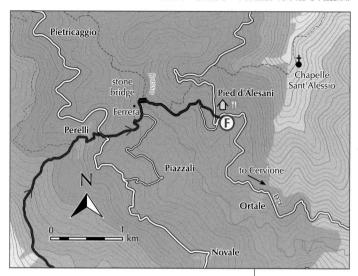

concreted lane, then fork R for the white stuccoed church that doubles as home to chattering swifts in the farming hamlet of **Perelli** (750m, **1hr**, drinking fountain, cheese and charcuterie products on sale).

At the École (school), orange markers send you on a knee-jarring drop via steps to crossroads on the D17/D217. Down at a chapel you'll need to hunt around for the faintly marked path that crashes through chaotic woodland, inhabited by woodpeckers and pungent goats. It cuts across a road before crossing a stream and following its bank to a road bridge. Turn L on the tarmac past a farm to the old mill at **Ferrera**, and cross the grey **stone bridge** (450m) over the wondrous gushing Busso river. A little way uphill, you're pointed L for a final stiff slog to a minor road leading into **Pied d'Alesani** (680m, **45min**, café-restaurant).

Signs point to the well-run comfortable council-owned *gîte d'étape* (tel 06 23743438, p.bat@sfr.fr, sleeps 16, open Apr–Oct, kitchen facilities).

STAGE 10
Pied d'Alesani to I Penti

Start	Pied d'Alesani
Distance	9.9km
Ascent	460m
Descent	530m
Walking time	4hr 10min

A long, enjoyably solitary traverse of rolling hills is undertaken, with a string of superb scenic ridges, before you finally embark on the drop to villages and accommodation. The paths are narrow and rough at times, but plentiful waymarking guides you well.

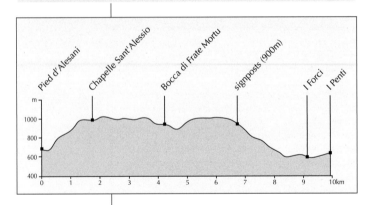

From Pied d'Alesani, orange waymarks lead via ramps and steps away from the houses. Up at a road and grey house, go sharp R twice and past a drinking fountain for a steep climb E through woodland bright with foxgloves to reach the **Chapelle Sant'Alessio** (960m, **45min**). ◀ A section NE with ups and downs features low maquis studded with scented wildflowers and accompanied by cooling sea breezes. Then comes an especially scenic ridge and

This is a marvellous lookout point to the Tyrrhenian Sea and the Italian islands of the Tuscan archipelago.

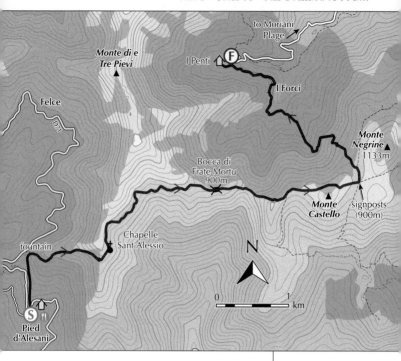

the col **Bocca di Frate Mortu** (900m, **1hr**), named for a monk who lost his life in a blizzard.

Soon the path forks. It doesn't matter which you choose, as the two ways quickly join up at a minor saddle for a stiff climb through trees, re-emerging on a brilliantly panoramic ridge overlooking wild wooded valleys and the glittering sea. Rock obelisks accompany you through to a grassy saddle (1020m) where you branch L via a low stone wall to continue along the left flank of modest Monte Castello. On a flat, open crest you find yourself facing the modest rise of Monte Negrine, absolutely smothered in broom. ▶

Here, at a batch of **signposts** (900m, **1hr**), you're pointed sharp L (NW) through hawthorn to swing into

In 1943, this was a strategic parachute drop point for arms and supplies for the Resistance, announced in code by Radio Londres.

On the way to Bocca di Frate Mortu

a side valley and zigzag down beneath chestnut trees, which give way to a jungle of creepers and vines. Further down, two concrete bridges over inviting rock pools with cascades need crossing, then it's up into the peaceful hamlet of **I Forci** (605m, **1hr 15min**). At the opposite end of the old terrace-style dwellings, a shady road takes you WNW to **I Penti** (615m, **10min**).

> Friendly *gîte d'étape* Luna Piena (tel 04 20573805 or 06 20018463, celinesisti@free.fr, sleeps 20, open Apr–Oct, cooking facilities). This final establishment on the MMN boasts a garden for guests and a lovely shady setting on an 'island' between streams and photogenic stone bridges. The village of I Penti, a tranquil, minuscule affair, is a mere stone's throw away and worth exploring.

> Back in the 11th century the Saracens were finally kicked off the island by the Pisans, and that's when the villages of **I Forci** and **I Penti** were founded, by people heading down from the mountains where they had taken refuge.

STAGE 11
I Penti to Moriani Plage

Start	I Penti
Distance	10.2km
Ascent	50m
Descent	660m
Walking time	2hr 45min

This short and straightforward final section concludes at sea level and hustle and bustle once more. Phew!

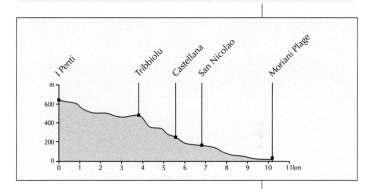

From the *gîte d'étape*, take the D34 downhill, ignoring the fork to I Penti proper. Just around the bend, take the path off R. It runs parallel to the road and passes scattered tombs before veering R and down to cross the stream, draped with all manner of greenery. Not far along, a river is crossed and you bear L (NE). A lengthy level stretch along the bank ensues via chestnut woods and lush green paddocks, eventually fording the unpronounceable Buccatoghju.

It's not far up to a drinking fountain on the edge of scenically located **Tribbiolu** (515m, **1hr**), which has towering slender stone dwellings and lovely views to the sea.

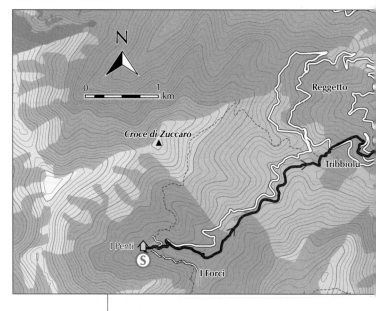

A marked track winds downhill, thick with wild mint and bracken. You continue in descent, and below a chapel an asphalt road alternates with a path for the remaining distance into **Castellana** (269m, **30min**), set on a brilliant terrace overlooking the glittering Tyrrhenian.

Turn L and continue through the village to where a path resumes in chestnut woods. After a water treatment plant, where the first cork oaks appear, you follow a lane through to the renowned Baroque church of **San Nicolao**. Take the marked way opposite the entrance, then soon fork L to swing back close to the tarmac. Go R at the next branch past houses to a well-marked series of lanes and roads leading into a residential zone. At the T-junction with a restaurant (I Lampioni), turn R for the main coast road, N198, and **Moriani Plage** (**1hr 15min**). ◀

The tourist office (tel 04 95384173) is immediately to the right.

Shops, ice cream, ATM, accommodation and year-round buses to both Bastia and Porto-Vecchio.

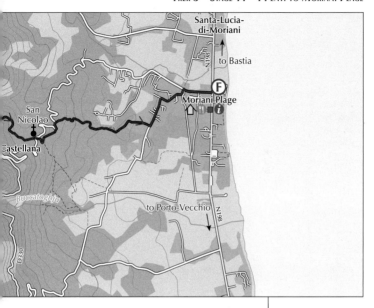

Moriani Plage might not be the island's most exciting beach, but it does mean a nice spot of sand to laze on after a swim, in contemplation of all those hills you've trekked across.

The sandy beach of Moriani Plage marks the end of the trek!

TREK 4
Mare a Mare Sud: Porto-Vecchio to Burgu

Start	Porto-Vecchio
Finish	Burgu
Distance	75.9km
Walking time	5 days
Maps	IGN 1:25,000, sheets 4254ET, 4254OT, 4253OT
Access	Porto-Vecchio lies on the southeastern coast of Corsica and is served by year-round buses from Ajaccio, Bastia and Bonifacio. To help with entering or leaving the trek at intermediate villages, there's a year-round (but not always daily) bus run between Porto-Vecchio and Ajaccio via L'Ospedale, Quenza and Serra-di-Scopamène. Further on, Sainte-Lucie-de-Tallano has buses to Propriano and Ajaccio.
Note	Avoid midsummer as it can get suffocatingly hot at low–medium altitudes.

> I have seen the southern part of the Island pretty
> thoroughly. Its inner scenery is magnificent – a sort
> of Alpine character with more southern vegetation
> impresses you, & the vast pine forests unlike those of
> gloomy dark monotonous firs of the north, are green
> and varied Pinus Maritima.
> *Edward Lear on his visit in the 1860s*

The Mare a Mare Sud (MMS) is a glorious coast-to-coast traverse of a great slice of southern Corsica, from the vast Golfe de Porto-Vecchio in the east over to the scenic Golfe de Valinco in the west. In between lies the ancient Terre des Seigneurs (Land of the Lords), with settlements dating back to prehistory. Nowadays it is renowned for its laid-back atmosphere and as one of the greenest regions on the island, with high-altitude plateaus for livestock grazing and the hospitable villages of the Alta Rocca region with their superb mountain

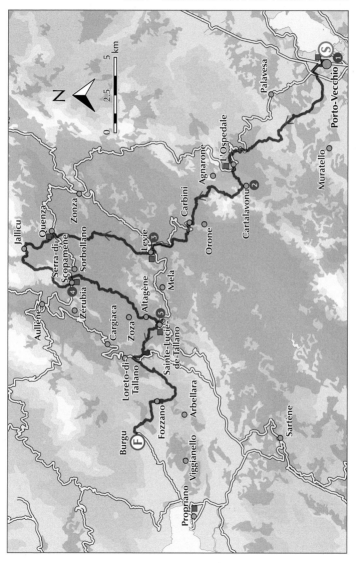

The red roofs of Sainte-Lucie-de-Tallano (Stage 4)

scenery. Apart from multiple river crossings – straight-forward in good conditions – no particular difficulty is involved, although the usual rule applies of being fit enough to deal with constant climbs and drops and an average of five hours' walking per day.

Waymarking is an orange stripe along with numbered *bornes de sécurité* (wooden marker poles), reference points for emergencies, and info panels about plants, animals and local history.

PORTO-VECCHIO

Porto-Vecchio is a lovely place to start the walk. Constructed by the Genoese in the 16th century as a rampart against pirate attacks, the town and its citadel stand high on a pink porphyry base overlooking a broad bay edged with productive salt pans. A rather touristy town, it boasts plenty of hotels, camping grounds, shops, cafés and restaurants, ATM and transport, in addition to superb white sand beaches. Tourist office (tel 04 95700958). Hôtel Le Mistral (tel 04 95700853, https://lemistral.eu).

STAGE 1

Porto-Vecchio to Cartalavonu

Start	Porto-Vecchio *gare routière* (bus station)
Distance	17km
Ascent	1000m
Descent	80m
Walking time	5hr 20min
Note	The trek begins with a 9km stretch of surfaced roads, some of which see little traffic. If desired, these can be avoided by taking a taxi (tel 06 26661301) to Alzu di Gallina, otherwise the bus from Porto-Vecchio all the way up to L'Ospedale.

This introductory day entails a steady climb through markedly differing vegetation bands, from aromatic coastal Mediterranean plants to the wonders of a superb pine forest on a medium-altitude plateau.

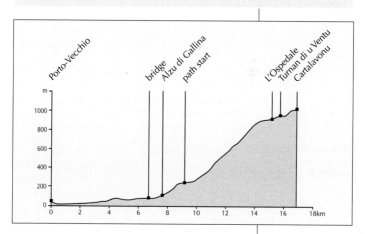

At the Porto-Vecchio *gare routière* (bus station) on the seafront, walk S past the statue of Pasquale Paoli then fork R for 'Centre Ville'. Take the next L and continue gently uphill, then go R signed for the Citadelle and tourist office.

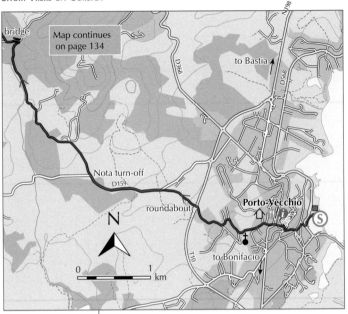

The tourist office is a short distance R.

Up at the ramparts, you enter the old town and go L along a shop-lined street to the crossroads Carrefour Simon Valli. ◄ Walk straight ahead on Rue Jean Nicoli and past Hôtel Panorama (closed). Through a residential area, the road lined with olive groves becomes Rue Daniel Agostini. At the Grimaldi family **chapel**, branch R, snaking your way downhill, then R again and out to the main road T10. Cross over at the roundabout, taking the Muratello direction. This soon feeds into the D159, continuing L (W) past rural properties and cork oak trees for 2km.

Go R at the turn-off for Nota, where orange way-marks appear and the cluster of buildings at L'Ospedale on the ridge comes into view in the distance. The quiet road leads over a rise with a white chapel-like tomb and on through woodland to an abrupt fork L over a **bridge**. Cross the bridge and take the next R for a grazing plain dotted with farms, before a gradual climb past

the scattered houses of **Alzu di Gallina** (140m, **2hr**) to where you finally leave the tarmac for the signed path R (labelled **path start** on map).

It's a gentle climb at first

A sandy path over rock strikes out through luxuriant aromatic maquis, starring lavender and native rock roses. You briefly join a broad track then climb to a **lookout** with sweeping views over Porto-Vecchio and its gulf. Maritime pines gradually gain the upper hand over the shrubs, and a dense woodland ensues, providing welcome shade. The MMS cuts across the asphalt road a total of five times (there's a café close to the fifth crossing) before veering L and onto a lane into **L'Ospedale**, aka U Spidali (880m, **2hr 45min**), where modest stone houses sit among a cascade of granite boulders.

Bar-restaurant, groceries, bus, *chambre d'hôtes* Uspitaghju (tel 04 95267753).

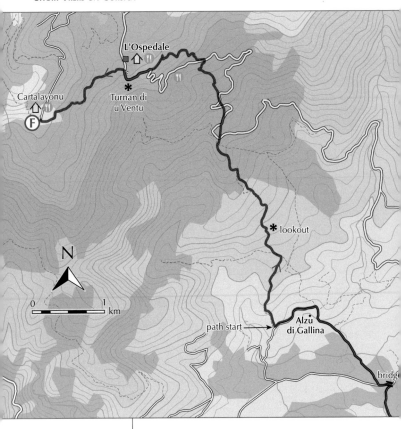

Join the road and follow it up to a café and fountain, where steps L cut a corner. Not far along is the stunning lookout **Turnan di u Ventu** (918m), with magnificent
views of the coast and over to mountainous Sardinia.
Only steps away, you're pointed L (SW) into the forest, a
cool dense canopy of towering pines and varied undergrowth of foxgloves and hellebore among huge boulders.
This restful stretch emerges on a lightly wooded plateau
housing **Cartalavonu** (1020m, **35min**).

Welcoming family-run *gîte d'étape* Le Refuge (tel 04 95700039, **www.lerefuge-cartalavonu.com**, sleeps 33 in dorm and rooms, open Apr–Oct).

Le Refuge at Cartalavonu

STAGE 2

Cartalavonu to Levie

Start	Cartalavonu
Distance	13.6km
Ascent	600m
Descent	1000m
Walking time	4hr 40min

Rolling wooded hills with occasional views characterise this second day, and there are several steep sections to test walking legs. Shady and cool best describes it. En route is an optional panoramic peak as well as villages with curious historical links.

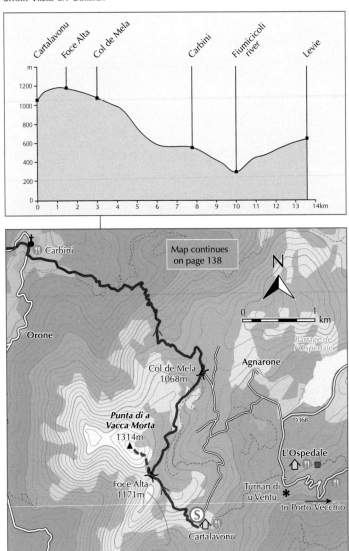

Leave Cartalavonu on the clearly marked path NW, climbing easily over rocks surrounded by rock roses, lavender and pungent everlasting. Orange waymarks lead you up a panoramic stone-studded flank bright with clumps of yellow broom. There are views to the Barrage de l'Ospedale prior to the junction **Foce Alta** or Bocca Alta (1171m, **30min**). ▶

A gentle descent NNE sees you at a minor road and the ample saddle of **Col de Mela**, aka Bocca a Mela (1068m, **30min**). The descent towards Carbini proceeds through pine forest, with innumerable zigzags and stone steps; clearly visible to the north are the Bavella rock needles, and hamlets and farms begin to appear below as the vegetation thins a little, with Mediterranean species such as holm oak and strawberry tree taking over from the pines.

After a short stretch of lane, it's L to cross a boulder-choked stream before an old way lined with mossy stone walls leads through to isolated farms. Keep your eyes peeled for orange paint stripes to finally emerge at the sleepy village of **Carbini** (560m, **1hr 30min**, snack bar).

> **Carbini** boasts a photogenic Romanesque church in Pisan style with a distinctive bell tower, dating back to the 12th century. Sadly, the site is renowned for the massacre of the mysterious 'heretic' Giovannali sect in the 1300s. Preaching and practising poverty, they were seen as a serious challenge to the church hierarchy, which led to their ultimate excommunication and untimely violent end. It is said that doves emerged from their funeral pyres and flew off towards the mountains.

Waymarking resumes opposite the church and you head for the far end of the cemetery before dropping to cut across the D59 road twice and plunging into dense woods of evergreen oak. An old sunken path W and then N in decisive descent concludes at the **Fiumicicoli river** (220m), crossed on a modern footbridge.

From here there's an optional detour to Punta di a Vacca Morta and some of the best views on Corsica (extra 200m up and down, 45min return).

The Fiumicicoli river is crossed on a modern bridge

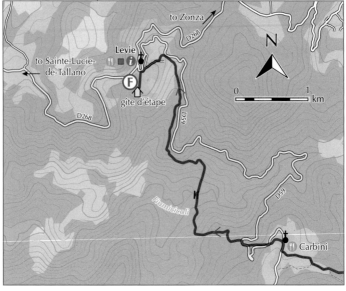

Now comes a steep, relentless climb through ghostly blackened oak trees, long-abandoned terracing and old stone walls. A traverse L and a stream crossing precede a final short climb past houses hung with roses. Up at the church you're pointed L past a cemetery to the well-served village of **Levie**, aka Livia (610m, **2hr 10min**).

> Immaculately kept *gîte d'étape* (tel 04 95784641 or 06 22312509, annauberto@sfr.fr, sleeps 25 in dorm and rooms, open Apr–Oct). Tourist office (tel 04 95784793), bus, cafés, restaurants and groceries.

> The local **archaeological museum** gives a good introduction to Corsican prehistory through finds from the nearby sites of Cucuruzzu and Capula, and also boasts a 6570BC skeleton dubbed the Dame de Bonifacio, the oldest human remains on the island.

STAGE 3
Levie to Serra-di-Scopamène

Start	Levie
Distance	18.4km
Ascent	750m
Descent	510m
Walking time	6hr

This magnificent if lengthy stage features a string of hospitable villages interspersed with wild mountainsides, rivers and rockscapes. For an enjoyable variant, take time out (1–2hr) to visit the fascinating Cucuruzzu–Capula Bronze Age settlements; afterwards, if time looks tight, you can always overnight in Quenza or Jallicu.

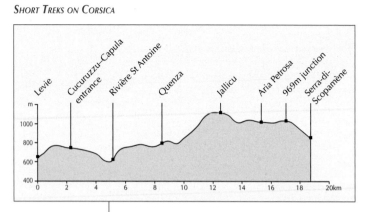

Walk up past the church to the fountain and crossroads in Levie, where the MMS heads up a concrete ramp N through the peaceful village. After a dip past a fountain, a delightful paved path breaks off L. Continuing N, it emerges on a grassy plain and turns R as a narrow surfaced road in sight of the wondrous Aiguilles de Bavella (Bavella Needles). Not far after a car park is the entrance to the linked **Cucuruzzu–Capula** archaeological site (760m, **40min**).

The broad cool path continues N past a pretty Romanesque **chapel** (St Laurent). Quieter now and shaded by a range of Mediterranean oaks and cyclamens, it descends very gradually between moss-ridden stone walling, past a branch for Zonza (ignore).

Proceed more decidedly downhill to cross a bridged stream in an area bright with orange lilies, to a prominent bridge over the **Rivière St Antoine** (568m). Cross over and head straight up the opposite side through tree heather to a fenced enclosure and a rough lane lined with heady broom. Keep R at the ensuing fork. ◀ A kilometre or so N brings you to scrubby woods and undulating pastureland with decent views to the Aiguilles de Bavella. You're led through woodland and across a bridge near a waste treatment plant before climbing to **Chapelle Ste-Marie**. Here, you veer R past ancient chestnut trees to **Quenza** (820m, **2hr 10min**).

Turn L for a useful shortcut to Serra-di-Scopamène via Sorbollano.

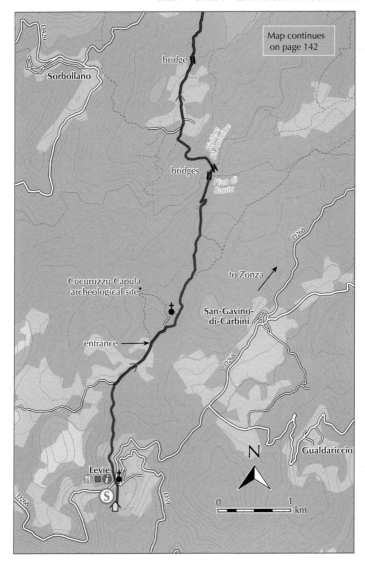

Map continues on page 142

bridge

Sorbollano

Rivière St-Antoine

bridges

Pian di Santu

Cucuruzzu-Capula archeological site

to Zonza

San-Gavino-di-Carbini

entrance →

Levie

Gualdariccio

N

0   1

km

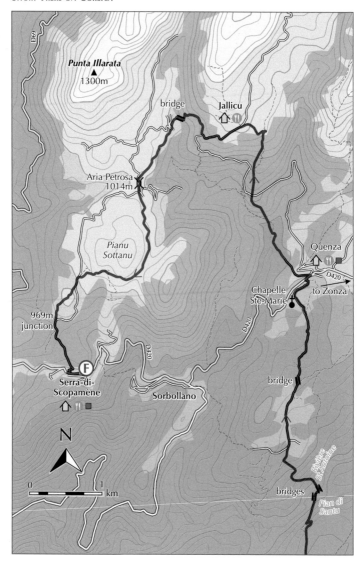

Punta Illarata
▲
1300m

D 69

bridge

Jallicu

Aria Petrosa
1014m

*Pianu
Sottanu*

Quenza

D 420

to Zonza

Chapelle
Ste-Marie

969m
junction

D 420

bridge

Serra-di-
Scopamène

F

Sorbollano

N

0   1
└─────┘ km

bridge

bridges

Rivière St-Antoine

*Pian di
Santu*

Accommodation at Hôtel Sole e Monti (tel 04 95786253, www.solemonti.com, open Apr–Oct, accepts credit cards) and *maison d'hôtes* Corse Odyssée (tel 04 95786405, www.gite-corse-odyssee.com, open year-round). Cafés, restaurants, groceries, bus, camping ground.

A signpost opposite the 11th-century church points you NW up a road onto an unsurfaced lane leading to a bridged stream. A series of old paths and lanes then climb steadily to cross the road near giant chestnut trees. Continuing steeply through woodland thick with holly bushes, you eventually emerge on the lower flanks of the vast Coscionu plateau. ▶ An abrupt turn L onto a lane leads through bushes of wild roses, aromatic thyme and everlasting, to the nearby road and scattered dwellings at **Jallicu**, aka Ghjallicu (1110m, **1hr 20min**).

This key pastoral plain is watered by a surprising number of streams, and punctuated by stone shepherds' huts.

Hospitable *gîte d'étape* Chez Pierrot doubles as a horse-riding farm (tel 04 95786321 or 06 01999037, sleeps 18 in rooms, open year-round, no cooking facilities). An overnight stay here really means getting away from it all.

The route sticks to the narrow road until signposting points you off R, plunging back into the woods. A **bridge** over a delightful cascading stream (978m) is the perfect spot for a cool rest; on the other side are stone huts in wild surrounds, dominated to the northwest by the rugged rock ridges of Punta Illarata. Cross over the bridge and bear SW to a col (**Aria Petrosa**, 1014m). Keep L (due S) across the Pianu Sottanu plain, a level expanse of heathland with an unusual number of spiky shrubs and scented pinks.

After a saddle there's welcome shade. Orange waymarks and arrows guide you through a maze of tracks to fields and a signed **junction** (969m) where you join a road S. Down at an elaborate votive shrine, turn L for the hospitable, panoramically placed *gîte d'étape* of **Serra-di-Scopamène** (850m, **1hr 50min**). A matter of minutes

The views from Pianu Sottanu are vast

around the corner is the charming village itself, nestling in the elbow of the valley, its cosy houses adorned with climbing roses and geraniums.

> *Gîte d'étape* (tel 04 95786490 or 06 62815247, lescopos@orange.fr, sleeps 26, open Apr–Oct). *Maison d'hôtes* Casa Sarrinca (tel 06 15447487, **www.casa-sarrinca.fr**). Grocery shop, café, bus to Porto-Vecchio and Ajaccio.

STAGE 4
Serra-di-Scopamène to Sainte-Lucie-de-Tallano

Start	Serra-di-Scopamène
Distance	10.5km
Ascent	400m
Descent	800m
Walking time	4hr

An enjoyable old way drops to a cooling river before a wooded ridge traverse that concludes at a memorable village. While it is not an excessively long day, stiff downs and ups make it rather tiring.

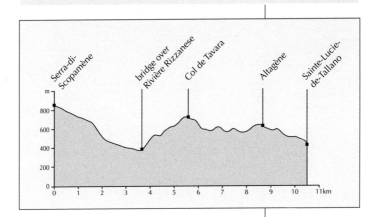

Head down the road from the *gîte* to the attractive village proper of Serra-di-Scopamène, where there's a café and shop. Not far down, you're pointed R onto a paved way dropping between houses.

Keep R at the first turn-off and follow metal arrows past an old chestnut mill. The delightful old path follows the line of the cleft valley with a trickling stream, ignoring a fork for Sorbollano. ▸ After a ruined hamlet, you join the D20 for a brief stretch downhill to where the path takes over again. A minor watercourse is crossed and its shady bank followed to a long **bridge** over the Rivière Rizzanese (380m, **1hr 20min**).

Majestic oaks and chestnuts along with abandoned fruit trees provide shade.

> The **Rivière Rizzanese** is a wonderful place for lazing around, although swimming is forbidden due to the dam and hydroelectric plant upstream. In any case, keep your wits about you as tales abound of mesmerising fairies enchanting local shepherds here…

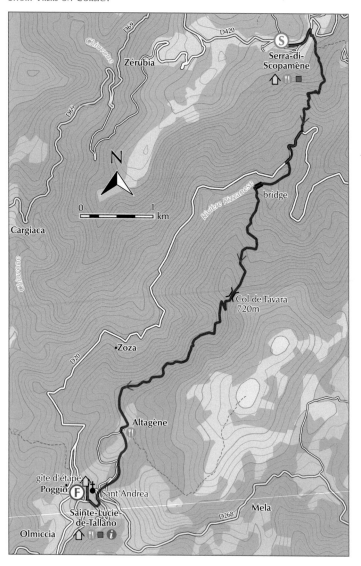

Of course, after the easy descent comes the inevitable ascent – a long one too! A clear path heads decidedly S through oak woods, climbing stiffly at times. Up at a minor ridge with views back to Serra-di-Scopamène, the gradient eases a little. Soon, at an open area colonised by bracken, the marvellous Aiguilles de Bavella come into view, then you gain the day's high point, the saddle **Col de Tavara** (720m). This is a good spot to rest, as an ankle-challenging descent on loose stones through dark woods follows – watch your step!

Two stream crossings later, the path improves considerably and you round a rock point overlooking the village of Zoza, backed by remarkable red crests. A level lane lined with giant fennel plants leads past a gate then a cemetery crowded with monumental family tombs. Over a bridge is the sleepy hamlet of **Altagène** (650m, **2hr**), sweet with the scent of lime trees, and a café.

At the road, fork uphill to where the MMS resumes its descent in woodland, shortcutting the road and touching on the **church of Sant'Andrea**. With the red rooftops of today's destination getting closer and closer, flights of steps drop the final metres to the marvellous fountain in

A paved lane leads out of Serra-di-Scopamène

the main square of picturesque **Sainte-Lucie-de-Tallano**, aka Santa Lucia di Tallà (450m, **40min**). Turn R here for a 200-metre stroll to U Fragnonu **gîte d'étape**.

Sainte-Lucie-de-Tallano has cafés with scenic terraces, eateries, grocery shops, bus to Propriano and Ajaccio, and rooms Chez Dume (tel 06 46713945). Tourist office (tel 09 88187911 or 04 95785633). The congenial U Fragnonu *gîte d'étape* is a 200-metre stroll from the main square (tel 04 95788256 or 04 95788013, **www.gite-tallano.fr**, sleeps 32 in rooms and dorms, open Apr–mid Oct).

The town name **Tallano** is believed to derive from either the Arabic for 'gift of Allah' or the Corsican for 'steep hillside'. As well as a number of churches and the derelict 15th-century convent of St François, it is famous for orbicular diorite, a rare stone of a curious blue-grey colour with lighter concentric rings, used for the Medici chapel in Florence. Curiously, the Corsicans call it the 'eye stone', while the town's revered namesake Saint Lucy (of Syracuse) is the patron saint of the blind.

STAGE 5
Sainte-Lucie-de-Tallano to Burgu

Start	Sainte-Lucie-de-Tallano
Distance	16.4km
Ascent	670m
Descent	1120m
Walking time	5hr 15min

Walkers embark on a strenuous day through wild landscapes with far-reaching views on this concluding stage, as the Mare a Mare Sud drops towards the coast.

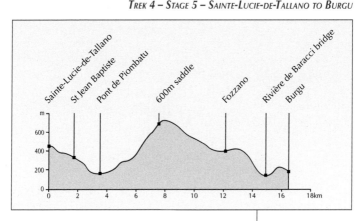

Leave the *gîte* on the path via the old olive press to join a quiet road heading R (W) for the houses of **Poggio**. Keep R at the intersection for a drop through extensive olive groves before coasting past the Romanesque **church of St Jean Baptiste**. A track is crossed and the waymarked path continues through woodland of broom and cork oaks in various stages of 'undress'. Down at the Rivière Rizzanese, the path follows the banks L to cross **Pont de Piombatu** (120m, **1hr**), a favourite spot for fishermen, where two pretty cascading watercourses join forces. ▶

A lane heads uphill, tending N through light ever-green oak woods and past a farm, to the D69. There, a leisurely lane L passes houses to a gate where a path breaks off up R through dense old woods, not far from a quarry. Maintaining a constant SW direction, it climbs steadily to open rocky terrain, eventually gaining the **saddle** close to **Punta d'Arja Vecchia** (600m, **1hr 30min**), with a ruined hut; marvellous views take in nearby Pointe de Zibo, the river and the farming plain below.

A further modest climb leads along a magnificent wild open crest smothered in heady scented lavender, cistus and pungent herbs. ▶ Around 700m in altitude beneath a prominent elongated rock outcrop, the way levels out and flanks an old stone wall, one of the many criss-crossing the hillside. Past a *source* (spring), a lane

Signs forbid bathing due to dangerous currents.

Sainte-Lucie-de-Tallano is due east now. The low maquis vegetation means there are good chances of seeing buzzards and argumentative crows.

149

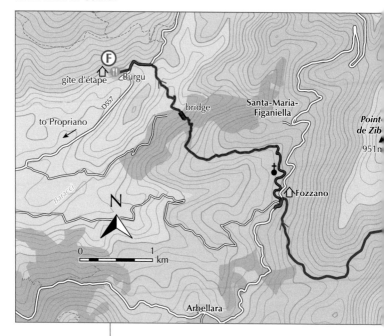

gives way to a path along a grazing valley, and not far on the glittering sea comes into view at last! The downhill amble proceeds through overgrown sections of shoulder-high plants, and you cruise into the pretty village of **Fozzano**, aka Fuzzà (400m, **1hr 30min**). Keep L down the road to an intersection near a grocery store. Chambre d'hôtes Maison Madamicella (tel 06 03833413).

> **Fozzano** is famous as the home of Colomba, a vengeful 18th-century woman enmeshed in a terrible tale of vendetta killings. Her story was adapted by French novelist Mérimée.

Follow orange waymarks carefully through the village with its historic towers and past the **church** on the road. The path resumes W at the next hamlet. After a

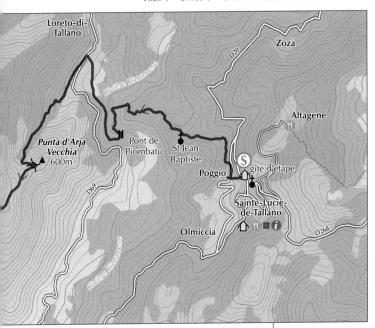

The lovely village of Fozzano

A ramble through olive groves once Fozzano is left behind

stream crossing, it's mostly level going via olive groves to a panoramic outcrop overlooking the Golfe de Valincu and Propriano. A gradual descent concludes at an old mill near the Rivière de Baracci and its **bridge**. An amble along the opposite bank gives way to a sunken way with masses of cistus and you emerge up on the D557. Turn L for the short distance towards the tiny rural settlement of **Burgu** (190m, **1hr 15min**) – don't miss the fork R to U Fracintu.

> Helpful old style hotel-cum-*gîte* U Fracintu (tel 04 95761505 or 06 11803141, **www.gite-hotel-valinco.fr**, sleeps 65 in dorm and rooms, open year-round, accepts credit cards). The panoramic terrace is perfect for a celebratory drink!

Burgu marks the end of the trek, but for ongoing transport and a wide range of services it's 7km from here along the Baracci valley into Propriano. Either slog it on foot along the road (about 1hr 30min), arrange for a taxi (tel 06 87222792) or embark on the Mare e Monti Sud!

> Propriano is renowned for plentiful accommodation (and traffic jams), and is good for a swim and a well-earned cool beer. ATM, shops of all kinds and bus services to Ajaccio and Porto-Vecchio. Tourist office (tel 04 95760149).

TREK 5
Mare e Monti Sud: Burgu to Porticcio

Start	Burgu
Finish	Porticcio
Distance	66.9km
Walking time	5 days
Maps	IGN 1:25,000, sheets 4154OT, 4153OT, 4254OT, 4253OT (the route runs along the edges of the maps; that's why four are needed)
Access	Burgu is 7km up a quiet road from Propriano (year-round buses to Ajaccio and Porto-Vecchio), in the Baracci valley. Either walk – allowing 1hr 40min – or take a taxi (tel 06 87222792). En route, the handy Porticcio–Ajaccio bus drops in at Olmeto, Porto Pollo and Bisinao.

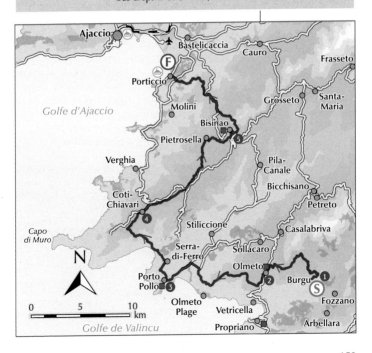

A rock outcrop means a view to Olmeto (Trek5, Stage1)

The rewarding Mare e Monti Sud links two major gulfs on Corsica's eastern coast, connecting the marvellous Golfe de Valincu with the Golfe d'Ajaccio where the island's capital shelters, backed by imposing mountains. It drops in on a string of attractive bays and beaches before climbing along broad ridges which double as magnificent belvederes. Accommodation is provided by a combination of hotels and *gîtes*.

Waymarking is orange paint stripes combined with low, numbered *bornes de sécurité* (marker poles), emergency reference points. Panels along the way provide interesting info about plants, animals and local history.

BURGU

In the upper part of the rural settlement of Burgu, where the trek starts, is the welcoming rambling hotel-like U Fracintu *gîte d'étape* (tel 04 95761505 or 06 11803141, www.gite-hotel-valinco.fr, sleeps 65 in dorm and rooms, open year-round, accepts credit cards). Its marvellous panoramic terrace is perfect for an opening drink.

STAGE 1
Burgu to Olmeto

Start	Burgu
Distance	10.6km
Ascent	800m
Descent	650m
Walking time	4hr

This straightforward opening stage begins with a stiff climb over wooded hillsides followed by a traverse to a great lookout, before dropping to a well-served village with curious houses that resemble towers.

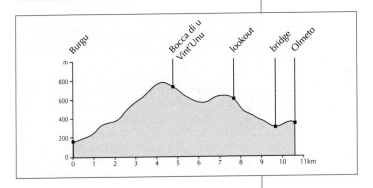

The actual trek start for Mare e Monti Sud is about 1km uphill from the turn-off for the *gîte d'étape* in Burgu (190m). The signed path breaks L off the road, heading NW through scented cistus shrubs in gentle ascent, with a gorgeous view northeast to red rock Monte Rossu. Join a leisurely lane L and follow it to where the path resumes N up a broad ridge in light Mediterranean woodland and tree heather. ▶ Granite outcrops appear around the 800m mark, today's highest point, and the way levels out, bearing NW to a small clearing with cairns – **Bocca di u Vint'Unu** (738m, **2hr**).

The steepish gradient is tempered by glimpses of the Golfe de Valincu, although the going is relentless.

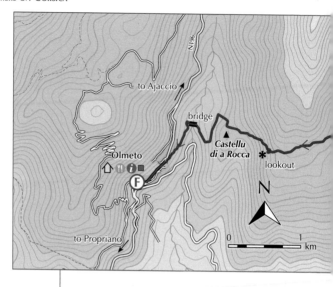

Finally in descent you cross a stream and walk to the ruined houses of **Vera** (553m), where a hut offers a sheltered picnic table. Now in ascent again, the path weaves its way between huge boulders to a magnificent slab **lookout** over Olmeto ahead and to the gulf. Watch your step for the rocky clamber down to woodland as the Mare e Monti Sud curves around the **Castellu di a Rocca** knoll before dropping past pylons and gates, finally reaching a concrete **bridge**.

> The stream here was once dotted with **water-powered mills** used to extract oil from olive pulp that had already been pressed. The resulting oil was shipped to Marseille for soapmaking.

> The ensuing ascent SW follows a delightful ancient stepped way lined with stone walls and flanked by olive groves to the road at **Olmeto**, aka Ulmetu (363m, **2hr**).

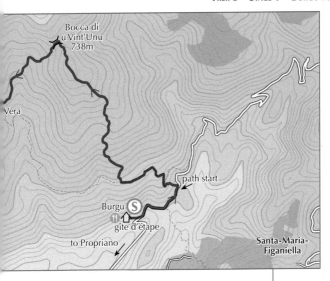

Tourist office (tel 04 95746587), cafés, restaurants, bus to Ajaccio and Propriano, groceries. Hôtel Santa Maria (tel 04 95746559, **www.hotel-auberge-propriano.fr**), Hôtel L'Aiglon (tel 04 95746604 or 06 17592426, accepts credit cards).

Olmeto on open hillside

STAGE 2

Olmeto to Porto Pollo

Start	Olmeto
Distance	15.3km
Ascent	350m
Descent	700m
Walking time	4hr

This lovely stage follows easy old paths on an enjoyable ramble with relatively little upping and downing, the sea providing constant inspiring company. A final stretch on tarmac sees the day conclude at the beautiful sandy bay of well-served Porto Pollo, where a swim is definitely on the cards.

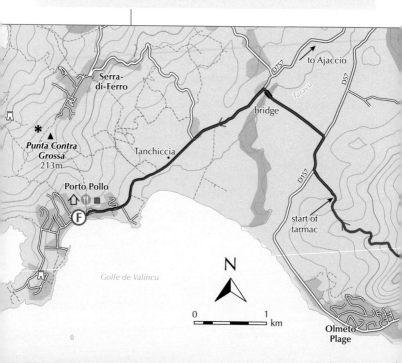

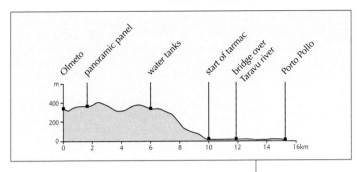

Leave Olmeto (363m) on the N196, heading down past the old fountain and Restaurant La Source. Turn next R uphill (sign for A Raghja–A Ribba) above the cemetery and stick with this road, enjoying views over the Baricci valley as well as to Propriano and its gulf. After a helpful **panoramic panel**, orange markers point you R onto a

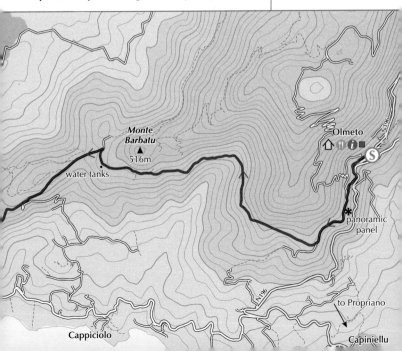

The surrounding ground has been dug up extensively by wild boar.

path. Heading through extensive olive groves, the beautiful old way lined with drystone retaining walls and ingenious stone steps has lengthy paved sections. ◄ At a power pole (379m), you join a lane for a short stretch beneath the rocky chaos of **Monte Barbatu**.

Shaped like a boat, **Monte Barbatu** was once an impressive fortified medieval settlement, although the site was occupied well back in the mists of prehistory.

Follow waymarks carefully past moss-ridden oaks through to two huge **water tanks**, used for firefighting purposes. Soon you veer L (SW) onto a quiet road; follow this for 2km past rural properties to join a lane which resumes NW. Flowering cistus shrubs and foraging pigs accompany you through a series of gates overlooking the lush farming valley of the Taravu river. Further along, a short but sweet descent sees you join **tarmac (2hr 45min)**. Keep straight ahead then turn R onto the D157 and follow it for 500 metres. At the ensuing intersection, go L across the grazing plain for a **bridge** over the Taravù.

At the next junction, it's L on the D757 for the remaining 3km SW. Along the way, yellow flags flower in the marshy land and the **Tanchiccia** nature reserve beckons to birdwatchers. You finally arrive in **Porto Pollo**, aka Porti Poddu (**1hr 15min**), a small-scale seaside resort on a beautiful bay.

The sweep of the beach at Porto Pollo

Porto Pollo is served by the Ajaccio–Propriano bus run, and has groceries and plenty of restaurants and places to stay such as a camping ground, Hôtel L'Escale (tel 09 74566429, **www.lescale-corse.fr**, accepts credit cards) and Hôtel Les Eucalyptus (tel 04 95740152, **www.hoteleucalyptus.com**).

STAGE 3
Porto Pollo to Coti-Chiavari

Start	Porto Pollo
Distance	11.5km
Ascent	700m
Descent	300m
Walking time	3hr 30min

This stage of the Mare e Monti Sud is simply superb, if a little tiring. After leaving Porto Pollo, it gains a panoramic ridge before dropping to a memorable beach. However, a taxing ascent over a further ridge awaits, concluding at the quiet village of Coti-Chiavari where vast panoramas are assured. Waymarking is faded in places so keep your eyes peeled.

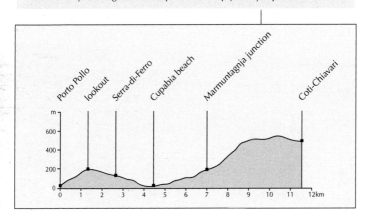

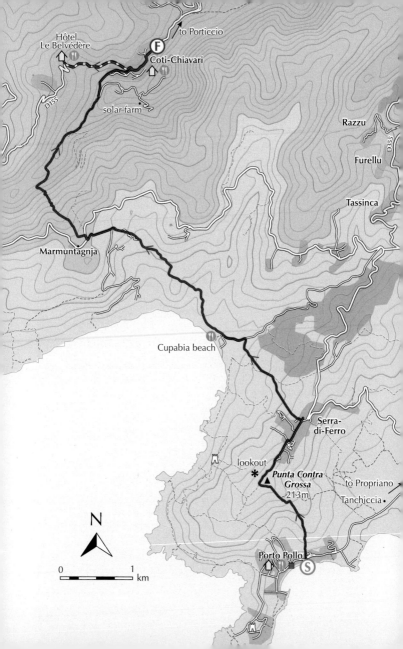

Hôtel
Le Belvédère

to Porticcio

F

Coti-Chiavari

D155

solar farm

Razzu

Furellu

D155

Tassinca

Marmuntagnja

Cupabia beach

Serra-
di-Ferro

lookout

*

*Punta Contra
Grossa*
213m

to Propriano

Tanchiccia

N

0   1
╠════════════════╣ km

Porto Pollo

S

Opposite the seafront supermarket at Porto Pollo is the signposted start of today's route. Old stone steps climb past prickly pear and lentisc shrubs then drystone walls. Flanking fields overlooking the Taravu river valley, the gradient eases and a superb **lookout** with a *table d'orientation* (213m) is reached. ▶

Further along, you join a minor road and head downhill to sprawling **Serra-di-Ferro**, aka Sarra di Farru (138m). After a hotel car park, you're pointed L for a shady path in descent NW between stone walls. At the bottom, it's L for a stroll to **Cupabia (1hr 30min)** and its renowned magnificent white sandy beach, dotted with strands of *Posidonia* and bright with yellow horned poppies (café-restaurants, camping ground).

Old watchtowers can be admired along with the gorgeous sweep of Cupabia Bay and its beach.

A **memorial** reminds passersby that here, at 2am on 11 February 1942, a British submarine dropped off three servicemen, who set up a network of Allied contacts to keep track of the activities of the Italians, who occupied Corsica at the time.

A boardwalk leads away from Cupabia beach

SHORT TREKS ON CORSICA

When you can drag yourself away from this idyllic spot, take the signed route via a boardwalk over marshland for the start of a constantly ascending path NW through the maquis. There's some respite at a leveller stretch by a farm, before the climb continues to a minor road and on to a junction near **Marmuntagnja** (182m). The path soon picks up L. Through alternating shady evergreen woods and flowered maquis, it steadily gains height. Around the 500m contour, it bears NNE to ramble along a broad ridge; the vegetation opens up, offering a wonderful outlook across the gulf towards Ajaccio and the Îles Sanguinaires. Wow!

A lane near a **solar farm** – with a good view over Cupabia and the Golfe de Valincu – leads towards radio masts to join a road. A short way downhill is a fork on the outskirts of the village. ◄ Straight on from the fork is the tiny village of **Coti-Chiavari** or Coti Chjavari (486m, **2hr**).

For welcoming Hôtel Le Belvédère, which is true to its inspiring name, branch L and head along the road for 1km (tel 04 95271032, www. lebelvederedecoti. com).

Restaurant, and *chambre d'hôtes* A Luna Rossa (tel 06 63398340, **www.alunarossa.fr**).

STAGE 4
Coti-Chiavari to Bisinao

Start	Coti-Chiavari
Distance	16km
Ascent	600m
Descent	400m
Walking time	4hr 45min

This superb if lengthy day begins with a leisurely amble along a string of undulating crests with constantly superb views. After the village of Pietrosella comes a never-ending series of plunges and climbs, and streams crossed on stepping stones.

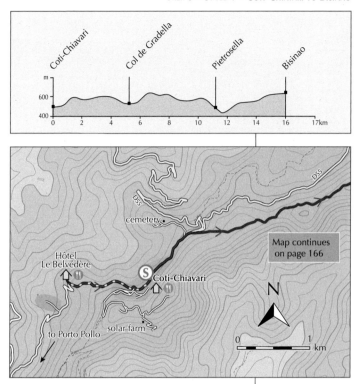

▶ In the village of Coti-Chiavari, walk past the Mairie (Town Hall) and restaurant and along the road NE. Soon after the fork for a cemetery (which you ignore), the path breaks off R up into cool oak woods, with granite underfoot. A mostly level ramble ensues, in and out of trees and past former charcoal-burning platforms. Marvellous views are a constant companion all the way to the road pass **Col de Gradella**, aka Bocca di Gradeddu (529m, **1hr 30min**), where there's a friendly café and yet more panoramas!

The path resumes N through clumps of scented lavender and tree heather, before passing cabins and following a stony lane lined with broom. A wide curve

If you stayed at Hôtel Le Belvédère, walk back up the road and continue into the village.

On the lane towards Monte Tignoso

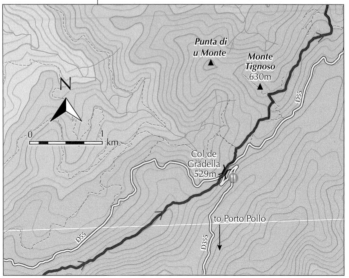

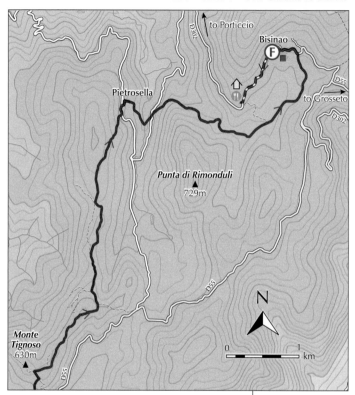

leads up near a pylon on **Monte Tignoso** (630m) then it's mostly downhill to a broad sandy logging track. Follow waymarks carefully as the route proceeds in and out of woods and past another pylon, before an old walled path finally emerges on a quiet road. You're pointed downhill to the village square and cenotaph of **Pietrosella**, aka Pedruseddu (480m, **2hr**).

Soon after, a path leads down R to a stream, which you cross on stepping stones, then it's uphill (naturally), cutting across a road and onto a rough open track in constant ascent. An abrupt drop sees you in a cool valley with a cascading stream and cyclamens, old mossy walls accompanying you E past impressively huge ancient trees. As you begin to emerge from the tree cover, the way forks – go L. After more minor stream crossings, you finally climb out at the roadside. A 10min stroll to the L are the modest houses and fountain that go by the name of **Bisinao** (632m, **1hr 15min**).

> The Ajaccio–Propriano bus run passes through here. Unfortunately, the *gîte d'étape* was closed at the time of writing, but luckily accommodation and meals are provided (1.5km SW out of the village) by rustic roadside eatery A Casa Nustrale (tel 06 63828240, **www.acasanustrale.webself.net**) and neighbouring *gîte* Sornagone (tel 06 43416673, **www.sornagonegite.com**).

STAGE 5

Bisinao to Porticcio

Start	Bisinao
Distance	13.5km
Ascent	350m
Descent	1000m
Walking time	4hr 15min

This is not a terribly exciting final stage to this wonderful trek, as there's lots of steep stony descent which can be tiring. However, lovely sea views are plentiful today and all fatigue evaporates once you reach the conclusion, the beautiful long white sandy beach at Porticcio, where lazing and swimming are in order.

From Bisinao, retrace your steps to where you joined the road E of the village yesterday, and continue along the tarmac for a further 1km to where the path strikes off L signed for Porticcio. You embark on a decisive climb N,

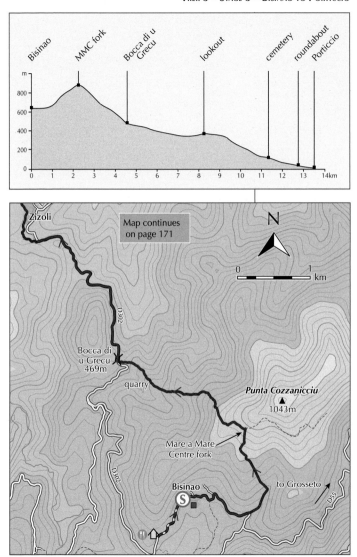

Map continues on page 171

The Gulf of Ajaccio can be admired downhill from Bocca di u Grecu

criss-crossing a stream and touching on long-abandoned terracing. Ignore the **fork** R (876m, **45min**) for the Mare a Mare Centre and keep L in the company of tree heather. Soon, a relentlessly steep plunge commences – take care not to slip on the loose stones. After flanking a quarry, you stagger out thankfully onto the road at **Bocca di u Grecu** (469m, **1hr**).

Follow the road R (N) for 3.5km, enjoying the outlook over an agricultural valley. After a stretch NW, turn off L on a lane, which becomes an undulating path through shady woods and abandoned fields. At a minor road, go L uphill then fork L at a **white house** for a lookout point with vast brilliant views over the Gulf of Ajaccio.

The path resumes N through maquis shrubs and trees. Further down, veer L past a house onto a pleasant old path heading mostly W. After a **stream crossing**, you reach a **cemetery** on the outskirts of Porticcio, with half an hour left to go. Down at a crossroads, go straight ahead past a tennis court to the main road D555. At the **roundabout**, branch L for the final metres straight through to the inviting beach of **Porticcio** (**2hr 30min**).

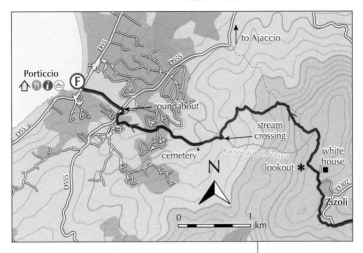

On the seafront where the trek concludes is the tourist office (tel 04 95251009) and the landing stage for an enjoyable trip by passenger ferry across the gulf to Ajaccio (tel 04 95210616, **www.muvimare.fr**), not to mention a string of cafés. Porticcio also has shops and accommodation, such as Hôtel Porticcio (tel 04 95250577, **www.hotelporticcio.com**).

What a spot to conclude the Mare e Monti Sud! The jetty at Porticcio

APPENDIX A
Useful contacts

The international dialling code for France is +33 and is needed for calls to Corsica from overseas.

Tourist information

Parc Naturel Régional de Corse
tel 04 95517900
www.pnr.corsica (in French)

Contact details for tourist offices in the principal towns:

Ajaccio
tel 04 95515303
www.ajaccio-tourisme.com

Bastia
tel 04 95542040
www.bastia-tourisme.com

Calacuccia
tel 04 95471262

Calvi
tel 04 95651667
www.balagne-corsica.com

Cargèse
tel 04 95264131
www.ouestcorsica.com

Corte
tel 04 95462670
www.corte-tourisme.com

Evisa
tel 04 95500687
www.evisa.fr

Levie
tel 04 95784793
www.alta-rocca.com

Macinaggio–Rogliano
tel 04 95354034
www.macinaggiorogliano-capcorse.fr

Moriani Plage
tel 04 95384173
www.castagniccia-maremonti.com

Porticcio
tel 04 95251009
www.ornanotaravo-tourisme.corsica

Porto
tel 04 95261055
www.ouestcorsica.com

Porto-Vecchio
tel 04 95700958
www.ot-portovecchio.com

Propriano
tel 04 95760149
https://lacorsedesorigines.com/

Sainte-Lucie-de-Tallano
tel 09 88187911 or 04 95785633
www.tallano.fr

Zonza
tel 04 95714899
www.zonza-saintelucie.com

Transport

Ferries
Corsica Ferries
www.corsicaferries.com

Moby Lines
www.mobylines.com

Promenades en Mer San Paulu
(shuttle ferry between Barcaggio and
Macinaggio)
tel 06 14781416
www.sanpaulu.com

Muvimare (passenger ferry between
Porticcio and Ajaccio)
tel 04 95210616
www.muvimare.fr

Buses
Corsica Bus
www.corsicabus.org

Trains
Chemins de Fer de la Corse
www.cf-corse.corsica

Weather
www.meteo.fr

Emergencies
General emergency: tel 112

Fire service (*Pompiers*): tel 18

APPENDIX B
Accommodation

Trek 1: Sentier du Douanier

Stage 1

Port de Centuri

Hôtel de la Jetée
tel 09 70356151
www.hotel-de-la-jetee-centuri.fr

Auberge du Pêcheur (hotel)
tel 04 95356014

Barcaggio

Hôtel Petra Cinta
tel 04 95368745
http://hotelpetracinta.free.fr

Stage 2

Macinaggio

Hôtel U Libecciu
tel 04 95354322
www.u-libecciu.com

Camping U Stazzu
(campsite with bungalows)
tel 04 95354376
https://camping-u-stazzu.jimdo.com

Trek 2: Mare e Monti

Stage 1

Calenzana

Gîte d'étape
tel 04 95627713

Hôtel Bel Horizon
tel 04 9562717

Bonifatu

Auberge de la Forêt (hotel/*gîte d'étape*)
tel 04 95650998 or 06 50775636
www.auberge-foret-bonifatu.com

Stage 2

Tuarelli

L'Alzelli (*gîte d'étape*)
tel 04 956213882 or 06 20484986
l.alzelli.gite.tuarelli@gmail.com

Stage 3

Fangu

Hôtel La Ciucciarella
tel 04 95332522
https://la-ciucciarella.business.site

La Casaloha (B&B)
tel 04 95344695
lacasaloha@gmail.com

Galéria

Hôtel Camparellu
tel 06 71971048
http://hotel-camparellu.galeria.hotels-corsica.net

L'Étape Marine (*gîte d'étape*)
tel 04 95620046 or 07 86046455

Stage 4

Girolata

Le Cormoran Voyageur (*gîte d'étape*)
tel 04 95201555
cormoranvoyageur@hotmail.fr

La Cabane du Berger (*gîte d'étape*)
tel 04 95201698 or 06 10230822

Stage 5

Curzu

Gîte d'étape
tel 04 95273170 or 06 22161593
www.gite-de-curzo.com

Stage 6

Serriera

L'Alivi (*gîte d'étape*)
gite.etape.alivi@orange.fr
tel 04 95104933 or 06 17559051

Stage 7

Ota

Chez Marie (*gîte d'étape*)
tel 04 95261137
www.gite-chez-marie.com

Chez Félix (*gîte d'étape*)
tel 72764956 or 04 9570649
https://gitechezfelixota.com

Stage 8

Evisa

Hôtel Aïtone
tel 04 95262004
www.hotel-aitone.com

U Poghju (*gîte d'étape*)
tel 04 95262188 or 06 80838647
gite-etape-upoghju@orange.fr

Marignana

Ustaria di a Rota (*gîte d'étape*)
tel 04 95262121
www.ustariadiarota.fr

Stage 9

Revinda

E Case (*gîte d'étape*)
tel 04 95264819 or 06 82499565

Stage 10

Cargèse

Hôtel Punta e Mare
tel 04 95264433 or 06 89724181
www.locations-cargese.com

Hôtel Saint Jean
tel 04 95264668
www.lesaintjean.com

Hôtel Ta Kladia
tel 04 95264073
www.motel-takladia.com

Trek 3: Mare a Mare Nord

Stage 1

See Trek 2 Stages 9 and 10

Stage 2

Marignana

Ustaria di a Rota (*gîte d'étape*)
tel 04 95262121
www.ustariadiarota.fr

Stage 3

Evisa

Hôtel Aïtone
tel 04 95262004
www.hotel-aitone.com

U Poghju (*gîte d'étape*)
tel 04 95262188 or 06 80838647
gite-etape-upoghju@orange.fr

Near Col de Vergio

Hôtel Castel de Vergio
tel 04 95480001
www.hotel-castel-vergio.com

Stage 4

Albertacce

Gîte d'étape
tel 04 95480560 or 06 17266706

Stage 5

Calacuccia

Hôtel des Touristes (hotel/*gîte d'étape*)
tel 04 95480004
www.hotel-des-touristes-corse.fr

Hôtel Acqua Viva
tel 04 95480690

Upper Tavignanu valley

Refuge A Sega (mountain hut)
tel 09 72661987
reservations at: www.pnr.corsica

Stage 6

Corte

U Tavignano (*gîte d'étape*)
tel 04 95461685 or 06 86902386
gite.utavignanu@orange.fr

Hôtel de la Paix
tel 04 95460672
http://hoteldelapaix-corte.fr

Stage 7

Santa-Lucia-di-Mercurio

Chambre d'hôtes
tel 06 88980292

Sermano

U San Fiurenzu (*gîte d'étape*)
tel 06 13178494
usanfiurenzu@gmail.com

Stage 8

Alando

Couvent d'Alando (*chambre d'hôtes*)
tel 04 95486421 or 06 38495349

Mazzola

Casa di Lucia (B&B)
tel 04 9359084

Pianello

Gîte d'étape
tel 06 08094433
a.casapieri2b@gmail.com

Stage 9

Pied d'Alesani

Gîte d'étape
tel 06 23743438
p.bat@sfr.fr

Stage 10

I Penti

Luna Piena (*gîte d'étape*)
tel 04 20573805 or 06 20018463
celinesisti@free.fr

Trek 4: Mare a Mare Sud

Stage 1

Porto-Vecchio

Hôtel Le Mistral
tel 04 95700853
https://lemistral.eu

L'Ospedale

Uspitaghju (*chambre d'hôtes*)
tel 04 95267753

Cartalavonu

Le Refuge (*gîte d'étape*)
tel 04 95700039
www.lerefuge-cartalavonu.com

Stage 2

Levie

Gîte d'étape
tel 04 95784641 or 06 22312509
annauberto@sfr.fr

Stage 3

Quenza

Hôtel Sole e Monti
tel 04 95786253
www.solemonti.com

Corse Odyssée (*maison d'hôtes*)
tel 04 95786405
www.gite-corse-odyssee.com

Jallicu

Chez Pierrot (*gîte d'étape*)
tel 04 95786321 or 06 01999037

Serra-di-Scopamène

Gîte d'étape
tel 04 95786490 or 06 62815247
lescopos@orange.fr

Casa Sarrinca (*maison d'hôtes*)
tel 06 15447487
www.casa-sarrinca.fr

Stage 4

Sainte-Lucie-de-Tallano

Chez Dume (B&B)
tel 06 46713945

U Fragnonu (*gîte d'étape*)
tel 04 95788256 or 04 95788013
www.gite-tallano.fr

Stage 5

Fozzano

Maison Madamicella (*chambre d'hôtes*)
tel 06 03833413

Burgu

U Fracintu (hotel/*gîte d'étape*)
tel 04 95761505 or 06 11803141
www.gite-hotel-valinco.fr

Trek 5: Mare a Monti Sud

Stage 1

Burgu

U Fracintu (hotel/*gîte d'étape*)
tel 04 95761505 or 06 11803141
www.gite-hotel-valinco.fr

Olmeto

Hôtel Santa Maria
tel 04 95746559
www.hotel-auberge-propriano.fr

Hôtel L'Aiglon
tel 04 95746604 or 06 17592426

Stage 2

Porto Pollo

Hôtel L'Escale
tel 09 74566429
www.lescale-corse.fr

Hôtel Les Eucalyptus
tel 04 95740152
www.hoteleucalyptus.com

Stage 3

Coti-Chiavari

A Luna Rossa (*chambre d'hôtes*)
tel 06 63398340
www.alunarossa.fr

Hôtel Le Belvédère
tel 04 95271032
www.lebelvederedecoti.com

Stage 4

Bisinao

A Casa Nustrale (*gîte*)
tel 06 63828240
www.acasanustrale.webself.net

Sornagone (*gîte*)
tel 06 43416673
www.sornagonegite.com

Porticcio

Hôtel Porticcio
tel 04 95250577
www.hotelporticcio.com

APPENDIX C

Glossary of French and Corsican terms

Transport

French	English
aller/retour	outward/return trip
autocar, car	bus
auto-stop	hitchhiking
bateau	boat, ship
car	bus, coach
chemin de fer	railway
gare	railway station
gare routière	bus station
navette	shuttle service
tarif	fare

Timetables

French	English
horaire	timetable
quotidien	daily
sauf	except
seulement	only
tous les jours	daily, every day
lundi	Monday
mardi	Tuesday
mercredi	Wednesday
jeudi	Thursday
vendredi	Friday
samedi	Saturday
dimanche	Sunday
jours fériés	Sunday and public holidays

Accommodation and meals

French	English
accueil	reception, ticket booth
aire de bivouac	camping area
auberge	hotel, guesthouse
bain	bath
chambre	bedroom
chambre d'hôtes	B&B with evening meal
coin cuisine	cooking/self-catering facilities
complet	full (for accommodation)
couchage	beds
couchette	bunk bed
demi-pension	half board
dîner	dinner, evening meal
dortoir	dormitory
douche	shower
drap	sheet (for bed)
en location	for rent
gîte d'étape	walkers' hostel
hébergement	accommodation
maison d'hôtes	B&B with evening meal
panier-repas	packed lunch
petit déjeuner	breakfast
ravitaillement	provisions
refuge	mountain hut
restauration	meals
sac à viande	sleeping sheet, bag liner
serviette	towel

Food and drink

French/Corsican	English
acqua, eau	water
alimentation	grocery store
bière pression	draft beer
boulangerie	bakery
buvette	snack bar
casse-croûte	snack
eau potable	drinking water
épicerie	grocery store
fermé	closed
fontaine	spring, drinking water
libre-service	self-service grocery store
ouvert	open
pain	bread
vente de fromage	cheese for sale

Equipment

French	English
boussole	compass
carte	map
portable	mobile phone
sac à dos	rucksack

Weather

French	English
météo	weather forecast
neige	snow
névé	permanent snow
vent	wind
orage	storm
pluie	rain
soleil	sun

Health and emergencies

French	English
au secours!	help!
coup de soleil	sunstroke
crue d'orage	danger of flash flood
feu	fire, signal station
secours	rescue
pharmacie	chemist
pompiers	fire service

In town

French/Corsican	English
casa	house
distributeur automatique de billets	ATM
école	school
église	church
Hôtel de Ville, Mairie	Town Hall
maison	house
office de tourisme	tourist office
point d'accueil touristique	tourist office
renseignements	information
syndicat d'initiative	tourist office

On the trail

French/Corsican	English
aiguille	rock needle
balade	stroll, walk
balisé	waymarked
barrage	dam
belvédère	scenic lookout point
bergerie	shepherd's hut
bocca	pass ('mouth')
bois	wood

French/Corsican	English
borne de securité	safety marker pole
boucle	loop
départ	start point
droit	right (direction)
étape	walk stage
facile	easy
gauche	left (direction)
capo, capu	cape, mountain
carrefour	crossroads
cascade	waterfall
châtaigne	chestnut
chasse	hunting
chemin	path, way
col	mountain pass
courbe	bend
couvent	convent
crête	ridge
croix	cross, crucifix
défilé	ravine, gorge
falaise	cliff
fleuve	river
foce	col
forêt	forest
gibier	game (animals)
grotte	cave
hameau	hamlet
île	island
lacets	zigzags
lavoir	trough
littoral	coast
montée	ascent
moulin	mill
muletier	mule track
passerelle suspendue	suspension bridge
pente	slope
phare	lighthouse

French/Corsican	English
piscine	swimming pool, rock pool
piste	unsurfaced road, lane
plage	beach
pont	bridge
punta	rock point
raide	steep
randonnée pédestre	walking
ravin	ravine
rive	riverbank
rivière	river
route	road
ruisseau	stream
sanglier	boar
sémaphore	signal station
sentier	path
sommet	mountain summit
source	spring (water)
table d'orientation	orientation table explaining a panorama
torrent	mountain stream
tour	tower
vallée	valley
ville	town
voie sans issue	dead-end road

APPENDIX D
Further reading

Top of the list is *Asterix in Corsica* by R Goscinny and A Uderzo (1973), which captures the character of the island in a delightfully irreverent manner. A close second is *Granite Island: A Portrait of Corsica* (1971). A serious read that verges on gripping, this is Dorothy Carrington's passionate account of late 1940s Corsica set against a web of spirits: 'Get away from here before you're completely bewitched and enslaved!' she was told.

If you have access to an antique book store, search out either of James Boswell's travel journals dating back to the late 1700s, as well as Edward Lear's delightful *Journal of a Landscape Painter in Corsica* (1870). Latter-day traveller Paul Theroux also passed through, as recounted in his very readable *The Pillars of Hercules: A Grand Tour of the Mediterranean* (1995).

Readers of French should look out for the mesmerising short stories by Guy de Maupassant, including *Un bandit corse* (1882), *Histoire corse* (1881) and *La Patrie de Colomba* (1880). There's also fascinating reading in *Contes et Légendes de l'île de Corse* by Gabriel Xavier Culioli (1998) and Claire Tiévant and Lucie Desideri's *Almanach de la mémoire et des coutumes: Corse* (1986).

Experienced walkers keen on the challenging Grande Randonnée GR20 which traverses Corsica will appreciate Paddy Dillon's guide *The GR20 Corsica: The High Level Route*, while those in search of day walks should turn to *Walking on Corsica* (both published by Cicerone). Plant enthusiasts should check out the beautifully illustrated *Wild Flowers of the Mediterranean* (2008) by M Blamey and C Grey-Wilson.

Lastly, for anyone planning a trip to Corsica, taking a look at www.corsicanow.com is absolutely essential – an insider offers his entertaining view of the island.

NOTES

NOTES

NOTES

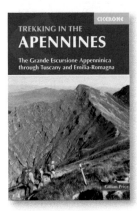
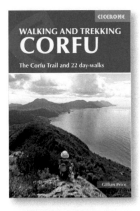
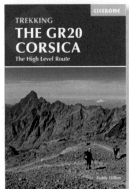
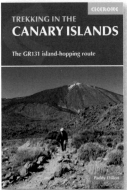

LISTING OF CICERONE GUIDES

SCOTLAND

Backpacker's Britain:
  Northern Scotland
Ben Nevis and Glen Coe
Cycle Touring in Northern Scotland
Cycling in the Hebrides
Great Mountain Days in Scotland
Mountain Biking in Southern and
  Central Scotland
Mountain Biking in West and North
  West Scotland
Not the West Highland Way
Scotland
Scotland's Best Small Mountains
Scotland's Mountain Ridges
The Ayrshire and Arran Coastal Paths
The Border Country
The Borders Abbeys Way
The Cape Wrath Trail
The Great Glen Way
The Great Glen Way Map Booklet
The Hebridean Way
The Hebrides
The Isle of Mull
The Isle of Skye
The Skye Trail
The Southern Upland Way
The Speyside Way
The Speyside Way Map Booklet
The West Highland Way
Walking Highland Perthshire
Walking in Scotland's Far North
Walking in the Angus Glens
Walking in the Cairngorms
Walking in the Ochils, Campsie Fells
  and Lomond Hills
Walking in the Pentland Hills
Walking in the Southern Uplands
Walking in Torridon
Walking Loch Lomond and
  the Trossachs
Walking on Arran
Walking on Harris and Lewis
Walking on Jura, Islay and Colonsay
Walking on Rum and the Small Isles
Walking on the Orkney and
  Shetland Isles
Walking on Uist and Barra
Walking the Corbetts
  Vol 1 South of the Great Glen
Walking the Corbetts
  Vol 2 North of the Great Glen
Walking the Galloway Hills
Walking the Munros Vol 1 – Southern,
  Central and Western Highlands
Walking the Munros Vol 2 – Northern
  Highlands and the Cairngorms
West Highland Way Map Booklet
Winter Climbs Ben Nevis and
  Glen Coe
Winter Climbs in the Cairngorms

NORTHERN ENGLAND TRAILS

Hadrian's Wall Path
Hadrian's Wall Path Map Booklet
Pennine Way Map Booklet
The Coast to Coast Map Booklet
The Coast to Coast Walk
The Dales Way
The Dales Way Map Booklet
The Pennine Way

LAKE DISTRICT

Cycling in the Lake District
Great Mountain Days in the
  Lake District
Lake District Winter Climbs
Lake District:
  High Level and Fell Walks
Lake District:
  Low Level and Lake Walks
Mountain Biking in the Lake District
Outdoor Adventures with Children –
  Lake District
Scrambles in the Lake District – North
Scrambles in the Lake District – South
Short Walks in Lakeland Book 2:
  North Lakeland
The Cumbria Way
The Southern Fells
Tour of the Lake District
Trail and Fell Running in the Lake
  District
Walking the Lake District Fells –
  Langdale
Walking the Lake District Fells –
  Wasdale

NORTH WEST ENGLAND AND
THE ISLE OF MAN

Cycling the Pennine Bridleway
Cycling the Way of the Roses
Isle of Man Coastal Path
The Lancashire Cycleway
The Lune Valley and Howgills
The Ribble Way
Walking in Cumbria's Eden Valley
Walking in Lancashire
Walking in the Forest of Bowland
  and Pendle
Walking on the Isle of Man
Walking on the West Pennine Moors
Walks in Ribble Country
Walks in Silverdale and Arnside

NORTH EAST ENGLAND,
YORKSHIRE DALES AND
PENNINES

Cycling in the Yorkshire Dales
Great Mountain Days in the Pennines
Mountain Biking in the
  Yorkshire Dales
South Pennine Walks

St Oswald's Way and St Cuthbert's
  Way
The Cleveland Way and the Yorkshire
  Wolds Way
The Cleveland Way Map Booklet
The North York Moors
The Reivers Way
The Teesdale Way
Trail and Fell Running in the
  Yorkshire Dales
Walking in County Durham
Walking in Northumberland
Walking in the North Pennines
Walking in the Yorkshire Dales:
  North and East
Walking in the Yorkshire Dales:
  South and West
Walks in the Yorkshire Dales

WALES AND WELSH BORDERS

Cycle Touring in Wales
Cycling Lon Las Cymru
Glyndwr's Way
Great Mountain Days in Snowdonia
Hillwalking in Shropshire
Hillwalking in Wales – Vol 1
Hillwalking in Wales – Vol 2
Mountain Walking in Snowdonia
Offa's Dyke Map Booklet
Offa's Dyke Path
Pembrokeshire Coast Path
  Map Booklet
Ridges of Snowdonia
Scrambles in Snowdonia
Snowdonia: Low-level and easy
  walks – North
The Cambrian Way
The Ceredigion and Snowdonia
  Coast Paths
The Pembrokeshire Coast Path
The Severn Way
The Snowdonia Way
The Wales Coast Path
The Wye Valley Walk
Walking in Carmarthenshire
Walking in Pembrokeshire
Walking in the Forest of Dean
Walking in the Wye Valley
Walking on the Brecon Beacons
Walking on the Gower
Walking the Shropshire Way

DERBYSHIRE, PEAK DISTRICT
AND MIDLANDS

Cycling in the Peak District
Dark Peak Walks
Scrambles in the Dark Peak
Walking in Derbyshire
White Peak Walks:
  The Northern Dales
White Peak Walks:
  The Southern Dales

SOUTHERN ENGLAND

20 Classic Sportive Rides in South East England
20 Classic Sportive Rides in South West England
Cycling in the Cotswolds
Mountain Biking on the North Downs
Mountain Biking on the South Downs
North Downs Way Map Booklet
South West Coast Path Map Booklet – Vol 1: Minehead to St Ives
South West Coast Path Map Booklet – Vol 2: St Ives to Plymouth
South West Coast Path Map Booklet – Vol 3: Plymouth to Poole
Suffolk Coast and Heath Walks
The Cotswold Way
The Cotswold Way Map Booklet
The Great Stones Way
The Kennet and Avon Canal
The Lea Valley Walk
The North Downs Way
The Peddars Way and Norfolk Coast Path
The Pilgrims' Way
The Ridgeway Map Booklet
The Ridgeway National Trail
The South Downs Way
The South Downs Way Map Booklet
The South West Coast Path
The Thames Path
The Thames Path Map Booklet
The Two Moors Way
Two Moors Way Map Booklet
Walking Hampshire's Test Way
Walking in Cornwall
Walking in Essex
Walking in Kent
Walking in London
Walking in Norfolk
Walking in Sussex
Walking in the Chilterns
Walking in the Cotswolds
Walking in the Isles of Scilly
Walking in the New Forest
Walking in the North Wessex Downs
Walking in the Thames Valley
Walking on Dartmoor
Walking on Guernsey
Walking on Jersey
Walking on the Isle of Wight
Walking the Jurassic Coast
Walks in the South Downs National Park

BRITISH ISLES CHALLENGES, COLLECTIONS AND ACTIVITIES

The Big Rounds
The Book of the Bivvy
The Book of the Bothy
The C2C Cycle Route
The End to End Cycle Route
The End to End Trail

The Mountains of England and Wales: Vol 1 Wales
The Mountains of England and Wales: Vol 2 England
The National Trails
The UK's County Tops
Three Peaks, Ten Tors

ALPS CROSS-BORDER ROUTES

100 Hut Walks in the Alps
Across the Eastern Alps: E5
Alpine Ski Mountaineering Vol 1 – Western Alps
Alpine Ski Mountaineering Vol 2 – Central and Eastern Alps
Chamonix to Zermatt
The Karnischer Hohenweg
The Tour of the Bernina
Tour of Mont Blanc
Tour of Monte Rosa
Tour of the Matterhorn
Trail Running – Chamonix and the Mont Blanc region
Trekking in the Alps
Trekking in the Silvretta and Ratikon Alps
Trekking Munich to Venice
Walking in the Alps

PYRENEES AND FRANCE/SPAIN CROSS-BORDER ROUTES

Shorter Treks in the Pyrenees
The GR10 Trail
The GR11 Trail
The Pyrenean Haute Route
The Pyrenees
Walks and Climbs in the Pyrenees

AUSTRIA

Innsbruck Mountain Adventures
The Adlerweg
Trekking in Austria's Hohe Tauern
Trekking in the Stubai Alps
Trekking in the Zillertal Alps
Walking in Austria

SWITZERLAND

Switzerland's Jura Crest Trail
The Swiss Alpine Pass Route – Via Alpina Route 1
The Swiss Alps
Tour of the Jungfrau Region
Walking in the Bernese Oberland
Walking in the Engadine – Switzerland
Walking in the Valais

FRANCE

Chamonix Mountain Adventures
Cycle Touring in France
Cycling London to Paris
Cycling the Canal de la Garonne
Cycling the Canal du Midi
Écrins National Park

Mont Blanc Walks
Mountain Adventures in the Maurienne
The GR20 Corsica
The GR5 Trail
The GR5 Trail – Vosges and Jura
The Grand Traverse of the Massif Central
The Loire Cycle Route
The Moselle Cycle Route
The River Rhone Cycle Route
The Robert Louis Stevenson Trail
The Way of St James – Le Puy to the Pyrenees
Tour of the Oisans: The GR54
Tour of the Queyras
Vanoise Ski Touring
Via Ferratas of the French Alps
Walking in Corsica
Walking in Provence – East
Walking in Provence – West
Walking in the Auvergne
Walking in the Briançonnais
Walking in the Cevennes
Walking in the Dordogne
Walking in the Haute Savoie: North
Walking in the Haute Savoie: South
Walks in the Cathar Region

GERMANY

Hiking and Cycling in the Black Forest
The Danube Cycleway Vol 1
The Rhine Cycle Route
The Westweg
Walking in the Bavarian Alps

ICELAND AND GREENLAND

Trekking in Greenland – The Arctic Circle Trail
Walking and Trekking in Iceland

IRELAND

The Wild Atlantic Way and Western Ireland

ITALY

Italy's Sibillini National Park
Shorter Walks in the Dolomites
Ski Touring and Snowshoeing in the Dolomites
The Way of St Francis
Through the Italian Alps
Trekking in the Apennines
Trekking in the Dolomites
Via Ferratas of the Italian Dolomites Vol 1
Via Ferratas of the Italian Dolomites: Vol 2
Walking and Trekking in the Gran Paradiso
Walking in Abruzzo
Walking in Italy's Cinque Terre
Walking in Italy's Stelvio National Park

Walking in Sardinia
Walking in Sicily
Walking in the Dolomites
Walking in Tuscany
Walking in Umbria
Walking Lake Como and Maggiore
Walking Lake Garda and Iseo
Walking on the Amalfi Coast
Walks and Treks in the Maritime Alps

BELGIUM AND LUXEMBOURG
The GR5 Trail – Benelux and Lorraine
Walking in the Ardennes

SCANDINAVIA: NORWAY, SWEDEN, FINLAND
Trekking the Kungsleden
Walking in Norway

POLAND, SLOVAKIA, ROMANIA, HUNGARY AND BULGARIA
The Danube Cycleway Vol 2
The High Tatras
The Mountains of Romania
Walking in Bulgaria's National Parks
Walking in Hungary

SLOVENIA, CROATIA, SERBIA, MONTENEGRO, ALBANIA AND KOSOVO
Mountain Biking in Slovenia
The Islands of Croatia
The Julian Alps of Slovenia
The Mountains of Montenegro
The Peaks of the Balkans Trail
The Slovene Mountain Trail
Walking in Slovenia: The Karavanke
Walks and Treks in Croatia

SPAIN
Camino de Santiago – Camino Frances
Coastal Walks in Andalucia
Cycle Touring in Spain
Cycling the Camino de Santiago
Mountain Walking in Mallorca
Mountain Walking in Southern Catalunya
Spain's Sendero Historico: The GR1
The Andalucian Coast to Coast Walk
The Camino del Norte and Camino Primitivo
The Camino Ingles and Ruta do Mar
The Mountains of Nerja
The Mountains of Ronda and Grazalema
The Northern Caminos
The Sierras of Extremadura
Trekking in Mallorca
Trekking in the Canary Islands
Walking and Trekking in the Sierra Nevada
Walking in Andalucia

Walking in Menorca
Walking in the Cordillera Cantabrica
Walking on Gran Canaria
Walking on La Gomera and El Hierro
Walking on La Palma
Walking on Lanzarote and Fuerteventura
Walking on Tenerife
Walking on the Costa Blanca
Walking the Camino dos Faros

PORTUGAL
Portugal's Rota Vicentina
The Camino Portugues
Walking in Portugal
Walking in the Algarve
Walking on Madeira
Walking on the Azores

GREECE
The High Mountains of Crete
Trekking in Greece
Walking and Trekking in Zagori
Walking and Trekking on Corfu

CYPRUS
Walking in Cyprus

MALTA
Walking on Malta

INTERNATIONAL CHALLENGES, COLLECTIONS AND ACTIVITIES
Canyoning in the Alps
Europe's High Points
The Via Francigena Canterbury to Rome – Part 2

MOROCCO
Mountaineering in the Moroccan High Atlas
The High Atlas
Walks and Scrambles in the Moroccan Anti-Atlas

TANZANIA
Kilimanjaro

SOUTH AFRICA
Walking in the Drakensberg

TAJIKISTAN
Trekking in Tajikistan

JAPAN
Hiking and Trekking in the Japan Alps and Mount Fuji
Japan's Kumano Kodo Pilgrimage

JORDAN
Jordan – Walks, Treks, Caves, Climbs and Canyons
Treks and Climbs in Wadi Rum, Jordan

NEPAL
Annapurna
Everest: A Trekker's Guide
Trekking in the Himalaya

BHUTAN
Trekking in Bhutan

INDIA
Trekking in Ladakh

CHINA
The Mount Kailash Trek

NORTH AMERICA: USA AND CANADA
The John Muir Trail
The Pacific Crest Trail

SOUTH AMERICA: ARGENTINA, CHILE AND PERU
Aconcagua and the Southern Andes
Hiking and Biking Peru's Inca Trails
Torres del Paine

TECHNIQUES
Fastpacking
Geocaching in the UK
Lightweight Camping
Map and Compass
Outdoor Photography
Polar Exploration
Rock Climbing
Sport Climbing
The Mountain Hut Book

MINI GUIDES
Alpine Flowers
Avalanche!
Navigation
Pocket First Aid and Wilderness Medicine
Snow

MOUNTAIN LITERATURE
8000 metres
A Walk in the Clouds
Abode of the Gods
Fifty Years of Adventure
The Pennine Way – the Path, the People, the Journey
Unjustifiable Risk?

For full information on all our guides, books and eBooks, visit our website: **www.cicerone.co.uk**

Explore the world with Cicerone

walking • trekking • mountaineering • climbing • mountain biking •
cycling • via ferratas • scrambling • trail running • skills and techniques

For over 50 years, Cicerone have built up an outstanding collection of
nearly 400 guides, inspiring all sorts of amazing experiences.

www.cicerone.co.uk – where adventures begin

- Our **website** is a treasure-trove for every outdoor adventurer. You
  can buy books or read inspiring articles and trip reports, get technical
  advice, check for updates, and view videos, photographs and mapping
  for routes and treks.

- **Register this book** or any other Cicerone guide in your member's
  library on our website and you can choose to automatically access
  updates and GPX files for your books, if available.

- Our **fortnightly newsletters** will update you on new publications and
  articles and keep you informed of other news and events. You can also
  follow us on Facebook, Twitter and Instagram.

We hope you have enjoyed using this guidebook. If you have any
comments you would like to share, please contact us using the form on
our website or via email, so that we can provide the best experience for
future customers.

CICERONE

Juniper House, Murley Moss Business Village, Oxenholme Road, Kendal LA9 7RL

✉ info@cicerone.co.uk   cicerone.co.uk 🇫🇷🐦📷